The Department Chair

The Department Chair

A Practical Guide to Effective Leadership

Christopher J. Jochum

ROWMAN & LITTLEFIELD
Lanham • Boulder • New York • London

Published by Rowman & Littlefield
An imprint of The Rowman & Littlefield Publishing Group, Inc.
4501 Forbes Boulevard, Suite 200, Lanham, Maryland 20706
www.rowman.com

86-90 Paul Street, London EC2A 4NE, United Kingdom

British Library Cataloguing in Publication Information Available

Library of Congress Cataloging-in-Publication Data

Name: Jochum, Christopher J., 1976–, author.
Title: The department chair : a practical guide to effective leadership / Christopher J. Jochum.
Description: Lanham, Maryland : Rowman & Littlefield, 2022. | Includes bibliographical references. | Summary: "This book offers a personal and practical approach to leadership within the context of serving as a department chair"—Provided by publisher.
Identifiers: LCCN 2021041611 | ISBN 9781475862515 (cloth) | ISBN 9781475862522 (paperback) | ISBN 9781475862539 (epub)
Subjects: LCSH: College department heads—United States—Handbooks, manuals, etc. | Universities and colleges—United States—Departments—Administration—Handbooks, manuals, etc. | Educational leadership—United States—Handbooks, manuals, etc.
Classification: LCC LB2341 .J53 2022 | DDC 378.1/010973—dc23
LC record available at https://lccn.loc.gov/2021041611

Contents

Foreword

The preparation of academic leaders takes time, training, commitment, and expertise. Since faculty first receive their training in research and teaching, they scarcely anticipate serving as a department chair. How many professors woke up one day in the third grade and said, "I want to be a department chair"? Did you accept the position of department chair without leadership training, without a vision for creating tomorrow's program, and without a clear understanding of what it takes to develop a productive department and culture? Most chairs do!

Academics typically join the academy in search of a professional life characterized by autonomy and independence. During their tenure as professors, faculty observe the stormy years of chairs and scathing criticism of academic administrators and wonder: "Why would I want to subject myself to such scrutiny and public criticism?" Thus, most academics are not willing to give up their professional and personal lives for one of servant leadership.

Chris Jochum's opening chapter presents a reality check for anyone considering administration. He poses critical questions and exposes stark realities of "becoming a department chair." Why do you want to be a chair—for the money, a sense of entitlement, the perceived power, or just because no one else will do it? The author is not trying to talk you out of pursuing a chair position, but to explore your motives to serve—motives do matter. From my own studies we found that of those who accepted the position for extrinsic reasons (e.g., money, power, prestige), only 25 percent served one term or less and left the position. In contrast, 75 percent of chairs motivated by intrinsic reasons (e.g., serving others, learning new skills, advancing the department) willingly served a second term. Granted, the transformation from faculty to chair takes time and dedication, and not all faculty make the complete transformation to leadership. In his book, Chris Jochum astutely challenges you to define your reality: "What's Your Why?" Ultimately, are you ready to lead? If so, *The Department Chair* book will not just guide you, but illuminate your journey to effective leadership.

Throughout my research and experience over the past forty years, I have found that transformation from faculty to academic leadership is both an inner journey (search for motivation, commitment, satisfaction) and an outer journey (serve others, advance programs, hire and promote faculty, students, and staff). The internal journey requires an emotional commitment to serve—and demands competence, enthusiasm, and dedication. There is truth to the saying, "It's difficult to lead a Calvary charge if you think you look funny sitting on a horse." Examine your motives for serving and decide how you can "make a difference." In particular, Jochum's chapters on Courage, Mentorship, and "It's Not About You" will provide you with astute insight into your inner journey.

The outer journey requires you to hone your skills so you can provide departmental direction, advance your people, manage conflict, and create culture. To sharpen these skills, the author offers extensive chapters and comes to your side as a colleague with tips and insights. Dr. Jochum's chapters do not get bogged down in academic jargon, but he gleans the wisdom from current leadership classics tested by his own practical experience as a department chair. The critical core of *The Department Chair* book delves into what I consider the necessary survival skills of a department chair—conflict, culture, crisis, and hiring. I am not aware of any academic leadership books that address the issue of department culture, rather they just bemoan the irretractable cultures chairs inherit. The department's culture represents one potential stumbling block of effective leadership, where policies and practices produce barriers and strong inhibitors to productive change. However, in the heart of Jochum's book he first acknowledges that culture matters (chapter 5), then, in spite of the culture one may inherit, shows how chairs need to assess the current accomplishments and shortcomings (chapter 6), and finally guides chairs on how to create a new culture that reflects the collective values and future aspirations of the department (chapter 7). Throughout these chapters, the use of "sensing interviews" (asking critical questions and listening intently to the responses) provides the groundwork for assessing where the department is and where faculty and staff may want to go.

The chapters on hiring provide equally brilliant insight into the hiring process. Experts contend that the state of selection in higher education is precarious at best. Why? First, universities and colleges have very little actual expertise in the selection process, at times leaving it to past practices or happenstance. Second, chairs themselves do not feel particularly competent in the skills needed—and find themselves gravitating to what may be urgent, but not important on their daily to-do lists. Finally, most departments and universities have inadequate hiring, training, promotion, and succession-planning systems. Symbolically, new chairs are "given the gavel" one day as their predecessor leaves the next day, instead of "passing the baton" by mentoring the new chair months before taking office and coaching them into their new administrative roles and responsibilities. Chapter 13 brilliantly illuminates crafted character-based interview questions and techniques for onboarding new faculty and employees.

The author's writing style speaks to me, drawing me in by using probing and critical questions starting in chapter 1 and continues through chapter 14. This final chapter addresses how to move on and mentor new leadership. It is imperative that our colleges search for department chairs with a sense of dedication and commitment, not just a passing interest. The time of "amateur administration" is over—where professors play musical chairs, stepping temporarily into the administrative rank to take "their turn." This is not a time for ill-prepared faculty to reluctantly assume the role of department chair. Professors become chairs with only minimal preparation and leadership training. Universities recognize and reward PhDs for becoming internationally renowned experts in narrow fields, not generalists to serve in leadership capacities. As Chris Jochum asserts, the skills and accolades faculty may have received as successful scholars and teachers will not alone create conditions to be an effective chair. This is a people position and unless you love your faculty, you can't lead. Too much is at stake to let your department's leadership be left to chance.

A careful perusal of this book cannot help but give one a sense of grounding on what it means to be a department chair and navigate the inner, and outer, journey of department leadership. Dr. Jochum possesses not only a mature, thinking, investigative mind, but he also has experienced academic leadership from within as a department chair. His text flows gracefully and interestingly. You will detect quickly that his "coin" of language rings true. "He has been there," you will say to yourself. As a former chair and dean for over two decades, I recommend Chris Jochum's splendid book without a single reservation.

A POSTSCRIPT OF PERSONAL ADVICE

To chair, or not to chair? For many, there are no easy answers concerning which way to turn. But, as the Cheshire cat told Alice, if you don't know where you are going, any road will get you there. Inevitably all chairs leave their positions. Will your next stop be back to faculty or on to higher levels of leadership? No matter, if you are contemplating serving as a chair position, consider this sage advice:

1. If possible, wait until you are tenured and/or full professor before you accept the chair position.
2. Accept the position for intrinsic reasons *early* enough to keep your options open if you want to move into university administration, but *late* enough so you have time to establish your research agenda, academic credentials, and personal credibility.
3. Find a confidant *outside* your department—and *inside* your personal life for guidance—and ultimately seek a coach to guide you through the initial white waters of leadership.
4. Separate work and nonwork activities so you can maintain personal and professional balance.
5. Create a golden parachute—negotiate an automatic sabbatical to regain currency in your discipline at the end of your administrative term.
6. Leave right by: passing the baton, not the gavel; crossing the finish line in a sprint; taking care of others impacted by your departure; and reflecting on your legacy.

Don't wait until you end your term to write your legacy. Start now: How would you want to be remembered by your colleagues? Did you make a difference? When we surveyed several hundred heads of departments in Australia, three themes emerged from their legacy statements: "(1) We advanced **our programs**—our department is in a better place than before; (2) We advanced **people**—faculty and staff were promoted; and (3) We did it with **decency**!"

If you choose to serve, Chris Jochum's book will be an invaluable companion on your leadership journey.

Walter H. Gmelch, PhD
Professor of Leadership Studies and Dean Emeritus
University of San Francisco

Preface

Serving as a department chair is not easy but can also be one of the most rewarding positions one can hold in higher education. Over forty years ago, leadership expert and author James Burns said that "leadership is one of the most observed and least understood phenomena on earth."[1] Yet, almost all of us, for a good portion of our professional lives, are influenced by the quality of our leaders.

I believe it's possible to improve people's lives by improving their leaders. Therefore, the primary focus of this book is to help those going into leadership positions as department chairs in colleges and universities. Nonetheless, the information that I share can be applied to almost any leadership position. In addition, as I used to tell my college students as they were preparing to become public-school teachers, any piece of advice I give you to be successful, I most likely learned through experience, which means I did it wrong and had to go through the process of figuring it out.

As a former public school teacher, college professor, and current department chair, I have been fortunate to have had excellent mentors and colleagues who have guided me as a leader, oftentimes steering me clear of potential pitfalls and, most importantly, always caring enough to provide honest feedback. Therefore, whatever I share with you is out of a genuine place of concern; it is my hope that this book can be of value to you and those you serve.

On a more personal note, I believe that leadership has little to do with our title or position and is defined by our ability to positively serve and influence others through courage, character, and relationships. Because of this, I would like to impress upon you the significance of the influence that you will have on other people as their department chair.

As a leader, for better or worse, you will impact the professional and personal lives of those whom you serve. Let that sink in. You will affect their lives, their well-being, their sense of purpose, and feelings of self-worth. Your actions as a leader will also impact their friends, family, children, spouses, significant others, and so on. Individuals and their families can be uprooted from their homes and literally move out of town and across the country because of one bad leader.

Think about it. Lives can be negatively impacted because someone either became a "leader" for the wrong reasons or never had the prerequisite character and integrity to begin with. My friends, this is serious business. I'm not saying that people will never leave your organization and, in part, attribute it to you. As I'll discuss later, every organization has culture-keepers and culture-killers and sometimes people are just not a good fit. However, when good people continue to leave an organization because of leadership that is either inept, ineffective, dishonest, or downright corrupt, it's a problem; if you're their leader, then the problem begins with you.

Unfortunately, despite being committed to and passionate about their profession, some people wake up each and every morning less-than-thrilled about physically going into work due to an environment caused by a poor leader. One bad leader is all it takes to destroy someone's confidence, to make them feel "less than" as a professional and as a human being. One bad leader can significantly affect the course of someone's life and even that of their family. The lasting effect of a bad leader can endure a lifetime. Trust me, the only people who benefit from bad leaders are realtors and moving companies.

Here's the good news. The enduring effect and true legacy of a great leader are also far-reaching and can last a lifetime. One great leader is all it takes to build someone's confidence, to make them feel significant, and part of something greater than themselves. One great leader can positively affect people's personal and professional lives. One great leader can be the necessary influence that helps ordinary people (which most of us are) and organizations accomplish extraordinary things.

As someone who has spent a considerable amount of time in higher education, I understand that some of you, due to your backgrounds and training, may expect this book to be very formal and research-based. While I certainly will draw upon research at times, please know that the purpose of this book is to serve as a practical guide to effective leadership within the context of serving as a department chair. Therefore, as you read this, I hope to come alongside of you as a colleague and mentor, offering tips and insight. The role of the department chair is neither easy nor is it meant for everyone. However, for those who pursue the job for the right reasons, it can be one of the most rewarding leadership roles in higher education.

As a leader, you're going to affect the greater organization and ultimately leave a legacy, be it positive or negative. You can be the leader who helps people have a fulfilling career and find purpose in their work. You can be the leader who mentors others, impacting them personally and professionally long after you are out of their presence. The choice is yours.

Christopher J. Jochum, Ph.D
Chair, Department of Teacher Education
Fort Hays State University

Chapter 1

Becoming a Department Chair

To thine own self be true.
—William Shakespeare

Why do you want to be a department chair? Why do you want to be a leader? Those who assume any type of leadership role, in higher education or elsewhere, should never underestimate the impact of the position. Serving as a department chair can be rewarding, offering the best of both worlds through working with students, faculty, and administration; it can also be very challenging. According to Gmelch and Miskin, "The department chair position is the most critical role in the university, and the most unique management position in America."[1] To underscore the importance and complexities of the position, consider the following:

- Eighty percent of university decisions are made at the department level.[2]
- Department chairs serve an average of four years.[3]
- One in five chair positions turn over each year.[4]
- Almost 65 percent of chairs will eventually return to the faculty ranks.[5]

Despite the importance of the position, most department chairs are not adequately prepared for the job. A national study of over 300 department chairs found that two-thirds did not receive any type of training upon being appointed to the position and among those who did, 72 percent received ten hours or less.[6] This is not to suggest that those who enter the chair position are not capable since they are usually tenured faculty who have proven themselves to be outstanding scholars and teachers in their respective fields.

Ironically, however, the skills and experiences required of a successful faculty member are distinctly different than those necessary to become an

1

effective leader and department chair. Even though accomplished academics are intelligent and effective communicators who can critically analyze and solve problems, these skills, while necessary, are not alone sufficient for chair leadership. Gmelch and Buller contend that "academic leadership is one of the few professions one can enter today with absolutely no training in, credentials for, or knowledge about the central duties of the position."[7]

According to Ruben, De Lisi, and Gigliotti, "There was a time when being the best among equals, a master of one's discipline or technical area, was the primary—sometimes the sole—talent-set regarded as necessary for leadership at a college or university."[8] However, the modern complexities of higher education demand an enhanced skill set, grounded in the tenets of effective leadership, which by itself is "one of the most observed and least understood phenomena on earth."[9] Therefore, the expertise and philosophy needed to an effective department chair, which is synonymous with being an effective leader, is complex and further nuanced by the traditions and requirements within higher education.

LEADERS ARE IN THE PEOPLE BUSINESS

Although this book will pose questions that will hopefully provide you the opportunity to further reflect on your personal and professional reasons for serving as a chair, before moving on, you must address what is perhaps the most important question of all: Do you enjoy and understand people? Leadership is a service-based or "helping profession" which means people are your business.

Chapter 2, "People Are Your Business," will address this concept more in-depth. However, pause and reflect upon whether or not you're a "people person." Do you enjoy spending time with others, getting to know them and building authentic, professional relationships, all of which requires courage and vulnerability? Please know that this has very little to do with whether or not you consider yourself an introvert or extrovert. However, as a leader, you are in the people business and like it or not, will always be a walking, talking advertisement for your department and everyone it represents.

Leadership is a service-based or "helping profession" which means people are your business.

Another critically important component of being a people person and building relationships is communication. Are you an effective communicator? Do you enjoy speaking in both small- and large-group settings to a variety of internal and external stakeholders? Are you able, willing, and comfortable getting up and speaking extemporaneously or off-the-cuff? A leader who is unable to communicate across a variety of settings is similar to a surgeon who faints at the sight of blood. In addition, effective communication is required to address conflict, which occurs daily in the life of a leader. In all honesty, it's extremely difficult to lead people if you are unable to connect with them through effective communication.

WHERE DO DEPARTMENT CHAIRS COME FROM?

Department chairs typically enter higher education as tenure-track professors. Because of this, the first five to seven years of their career require being somewhat obsessive about scholarship, teaching, and service; it's important for others to deem their work worthy. For example, to publish a manuscript, one must convince peer reviewers that their work is timely, well-written, and contributes to their respective field. To have their articles published and grants awarded, other people must like their work, which some could interpret as respecting who they are as professionals.

As teachers, student evaluations play a large part in determining pedagogical effectiveness, despite their questionable ability to effectively measure instruction. As a result, college professors spend a good part of their time being somewhat cognizant of the fact that students need to like them or at least not despise them to the point of submitting scathing evaluations that will grab the attention of administrators and ultimately, a promotion and tenure committee.

Finally, tenure-track professors must provide service. However, what does quality service in higher education really look like? What would have to happen for an individual to be deemed unacceptable in this area? More than likely, they would either fail to serve on various committees or be so unprofessional while on these committees that colleagues would complain. Accordingly, this infers that in order to have quality service, professors must be liked by those in the department, college, and university.

Those who have gone through the promotion and tenure process can relate to the feeling of being under a microscope. During the pre-tenure years it's common to be afraid to truly express your opinions and unknowingly offend a colleague for fear that they might serve on one of your promotion and tenure committees in the future.

Not only do tenure-track faculty members spend a large part of their time making sure they are liked, but the process inherently requires them to be somewhat private and selfish. This is not to be rude or condemn the concept of promotion and tenure for those who work so hard to achieve this great honor. Nonetheless, being a successful scholar, teacher, and colleague often-times requires people to focus a great deal on themselves first and others second. It's neither bad nor an indictment of the individuals; it's just how it is.

How Are Department Chairs Hired?

However, as is the custom in higher education (because there's no other choice), when it's time to appoint or hire a department chair, people imme-diately look to the "super star" professors who have an excellent record of scholarship, who have secured millions of dollars in grants and external fund-ing, and whom, generally, most people in the department and across campus like and consider a good colleague. In other words, hiring committees make the common, yet flawed, assumption that a successful professor naturally equates to an effective leader. This is compounded by the fact that usually the new chair will receive little to no training, essentially being left to learn on the job.

Even though most people go into the chair position with little to no train-ing, they still accept the responsibility with the best of intentions. A survey of over 2,000 department chairs found, in ranked order, the top three reasons for serving in the position:[10]

1. To make a difference.
2. To shape the direction of the department.
3. Because no one else wanted the job.

The good news is that it's possible to acquire many of the skills necessary to become an effective department chair and leader. However, the process requires a great deal of honesty and self-reflection because the cost of poor leadership is simply too high—for you and those you lead. Therefore, before exploring legitimate and noble reasons for leading as a department chair, such as making a difference and shaping the direction of the department, it's important to acknowledge reasons why you should not pursue the position.

AVOID THE FOOLISH FOUR—WHY NOT TO LEAD

Below is a compilation of four predominant reasons for which people should not pursue a chair position. Please note that if you find any of these reasons are (or were) your primary motivation for becoming a leader, all is not lost. Unknowingly pursuing the chair position for the wrong reasons doesn't neces-sarily mean you are unfit to lead; it just means you may need to reexamine your true intentions from a different perspective. In the end, however, pursuing the chair position for the wrong reasons could mean you're in the wrong position.

> Pursuing the chair position for the wrong reasons means you're in the wrong position.

REASON 1: NO ONE ELSE WANTED THE JOB

As previously mentioned, one of the top three reasons chairs said they took the job was because no one else wanted to do it. Therefore, don't begrudgingly accept the awesome responsibility of serving others as their chair simply because no one else wanted the job. Would you want to be led by and follow someone who wasn't fully committed to the position, which includes serving students and faculty?

Unfortunately, most people can reflect upon their careers and identify leaders who only assumed the role because no one else wanted it. Taking a leadership position that has been less than desirable or even a revolving door isn't necessarily bad, if you do so for the right reasons. However, if you only accept a leadership position because no one else wanted it, those whom you serve will know you are in it for the wrong reasons and ultimately, you may not be entirely happy with the position.

REASON 2: POWER AND CONTROL

As a leader, you will have two kinds of power: inherent and earned. While earned power comes with time and is primarily the result of building relationships, inherent power comes immediately by virtue of your title and position. You're the boss and there are some things that you will control, regardless of your character, integrity, or reasons for leading.

Like money, by itself, power isn't bad as long as it is not abused. However, you should not pursue a leadership position if your primary motivation is to be important, have power or try to compensate for some unresolved personal issues or trauma. Most people would gladly accept the pay raise and put another title on their business card to be important or powerful; fewer people are truly willing to make the sacrifices and do the work to become an effective, courageous leader.

Leadership is a verb, not a noun; most people want the title but few want to do the work. The fact that you are reading this book shows that you have too much integrity to pursue a leadership position for selfish reasons or to simply control others. You're better than that. Besides, as a leader, those whom you serve will always see your faults, whether you realize it or not. As bestselling author and leadership expert John Maxwell says, "In most cases, those who want power probably shouldn't have it, those who enjoy it probably do so for the wrong reasons, and those who want most to hold on to it don't understand that it's only temporary."[11]

REASON 3: THE MONEY

There is nothing wrong with having goals that require a certain level of financial stability. Money is a necessary fuel for people's daily lives and it's perfectly fine, in part, to pursue a job because of financial gain and security. However, do not pursue a leadership position if the primary motivation for doing so is the money. As soon as you make your leadership position more about the money than the people and the purpose, your salary becomes the cost of your soul.

Granted, it's common for those in higher education who are not in leadership positions to regularly express concerns about the discrepancy between administrative salaries and that of the faculty. They use terms like "administrative bloat" and, somewhat in jest, claim that they could do an equally bad job for half the amount of the salaries given to the dean, provost, or president.

> As soon as you make your leadership position more about the money than the people and the purpose, your salary becomes the cost of your soul.

At the same time, however, you should not have to apologize for your salary if you pursue the job for the right reasons; the only thing more expensive than a good leader is a bad one. For example, what's the cost of great people leaving the organization due to poor leadership? What's the cost of a damaged public reputation, especially among students, donors, and alumni? What's the cost, both financial and otherwise, of litigation due to negligence or poor character? Therefore, as an effective leader, acknowledge that you are worth your compensation—just don't make that the only reason you pursue the position.

REASON 4: ENTITLEMENT

Abraham Lincoln once said, "You have to do your own growing, no matter how tall your grandfather was."[12] Regardless of how successful someone was as a faculty member, no one is automatically entitled to a leadership position. For example, in higher education, just because someone has earned full professor, given years of service to an institution, has published numerous articles and books, and has received millions of dollars in grants, does not, by itself, mean they are entitled to a leadership position.

Instead, ask yourself what you've done to earn—not deserve—the right to lead and serve others with courage, compassion, honesty, and integrity. What have you done to earn the right to ensure that most days, you are not the most important person on your agenda? Are you truly committed to making leadership your new area of expertise or do you see the chair position as a "thank you" job or "preretirement" gift for time served as a professor?

WHAT'S YOUR MISSION STATEMENT?

In 2009, Simon Sinek gave an inspirational TED Talk which has since been viewed by millions of people throughout the world. In his presentation, *Why Great Leaders Inspire Action*, Sinek says, "People don't buy what you do; they buy why you do it and what you do simply proves what you believe."[13] Sinek goes on to share his *Golden Circle*, which is similar to a bull's eye, with the outer circle representing "what," the middle circle is "how," and the inner circle is "why." This example is relevant to leadership and can be drawn upon as a framework for identifying your true purpose and passion, which hopefully involves leading others.

Looking at most organizations, the "what" and the "how" are oftentimes similar. For example, colleges and universities share many similarities in terms of what makes up a bachelor's degree, how and when classes are offered, how students earn grades, and how degrees are ultimately conferred. In fact, various accreditation bodies within the United States essentially require that institutions of higher education adhere to, assess, and report common guidelines.

However, most people would still agree that while there are similarities across universities and their respective academic departments, there are also unique, defining traits that make them stand out. Even though universities and departments may share the same "what" (classes and degrees) and "how" (how to obtain the degrees) their mission, their "why," is unique.

Why do you want to lead as a department chair? Does leading an academic department lie at the intersection of your passion and purpose? In their book *Find Your Why: A Practical Guide to Discovering Purpose for You or Your Team*,[14] Simon Sinek and his colleagues provide an excellent overview of how individuals and groups can better determine and ultimately create their purpose or mission statements, using the following format:

• *To_____so that_____.*[15]

"The first blank represents the *contribution* you make to the lives of others. The second blank represents the *impact* of your contribution."[16]

For example, a general mission statement for a department chair could be "to serve faculty and staff with courage, character and compassion so that they can serve students." Take time to identify the words that capture what it is you hope to do and accomplish and, most importantly, for whom. Additionally, think about what your actions, through effective, influential leadership, will enable others to accomplish and/or become. While your mission statement might change as you progress through your career, use it as a touchstone or anchor for your decisions, ensuring that, despite the cost or conflict, you are always leading in a way that is consistent with your values, vision, purpose, and character.

DEFINE REALITY FOR YOURSELF AND OTHERS

According to leadership author Max De Pree, "The first responsibility of a leader is to define reality."[17] Whether or not you are considering a chair position or if you are already on the job, you must be honest and define the current reality for yourself and those you serve. To do this, consider the following questions:

• How do you define leadership?
• Are you an intuitive leader?
• Are you comfortable with conflict?
• Can you define your resignation and termination?

How Do You Define Leadership?

How do you define leadership? What does it look like when it is and isn't effective? You should strive to define leadership as thoroughly as you would a concept within your chosen academic field because as soon as you become the department chair, leadership is your new area of expertise.

A person's leadership definition and philosophy can evolve over time as they gain more experience (i.e., make mistakes and figure out how to do it better the next time). However, it's worthwhile to take time to reflect and articulate your thoughts on leadership prior to assuming the chair position. Doing so establishes your foundation, acting as both a compass and rudder upon which you can base decisions, especially during difficult times.

Are You an Intuitive Leader?

Every person has their own unique gifts and talents and one way to uncover these is to identify areas in which people are naturally intuitive. This isn't to say that people cannot learn new skills and excel in areas outside of their comfort zone but it's always easier to enhance strength instead of weakness. For example, if you were asked to get up and give a TED-style talk with only fifteen minutes to prepare, what would you talk about? Typically, with little time to prepare, most people might regress to their comfort zone, which can also reveal their true passion, interests, expertise, and areas of intuition.

Identifying your areas of intuition and the extent to which it naturally intersects or coincides with your leadership philosophy can reveal your level of preparedness for the job. You don't have to be perfect from the first day because no one is. However, if you find that your areas of intuition and expertise (the title of your TED-style talk) are significantly removed from both the technical, philosophical, and personal requirements of the chair position, it might be an indication that you need to grow in a few areas or reconsider the job altogether.

Are You Comfortable with Conflict?

How do you feel about addressing conflict and having difficult conversations? If you can't address conflict consistently and without bias, you can't lead. Remember, people and all that comes with them are your new business and people can be messy. As Max Lucado says, "Conflict is inevitable but combat is optional."[18] Although conflict can have a negative connotation, when approached correctly, it can be a constructive growth component for organizations, serving as a means to renegotiate the terms of individual and group relationships.

Just as firefighters are trained to go into burning buildings while others are running out of them, as a leader, you must become comfortable with the uncomfortable. Addressing conflict and having difficult conversations, while not pleasant and normal to most people, are a natural, daily aspect of your job. Leadership is a service-based profession and each time you "run to conflict" you're helping the entire organization. As bestselling author and vulnerability researcher Brené Brown says, you must be willing to lead courageously, always choosing "courage over comfort."[19]

As a leader, you must become comfortable with the uncomfortable.

Can You Define Your Resignation and Termination?

Do you know what you're willing to resign over or be fired for? This may seem a bit harsh and hopefully will never come to fruition but, nonetheless, you need to honestly answer this question before assuming any leadership position. As a department chair, you will be faced with difficult decisions, requests, and temptations that were not even on your radar as a faculty member. You'll be confronted with adversity each day and as nineteenth-century novelist James Lane Allen said, "Adversity does not build character, it reveals it."[20] Therefore, think about your "non-negotiables," which represent those things that you refuse to do or be a part of, regardless of the consequences. Ironically, sometimes the consequence of doing the right thing and being a courageous leader can be losing favor with your supervisors or even jeopardizing your job.

ARE YOU WILLING TO START OVER?

In addition to thinking about the previous questions, it's also important to ask yourself if you're willing to start over by accepting a chair position, acknowledging that what got you "here" as a faculty member won't necessarily "get you there" as a leader. While it is necessary to have been a faculty member, preferably tenured, prior to assuming the chair job, the day-to-day duties and lifestyle can be significantly different. In addition to the aforementioned reasons to not pursue a chair position, consider the following:

- Have you paid your dues without being "due"?
- What is your leadership philosophy?
- Are you ready to learn?

Paying Dues vs Being Due

It's clear that most people are not adequately prepared (at least by their institutions) for the move from faculty member to department chair and cannot simply rely on past success. However, as previously mentioned, it's important to pursue the chair position for the right reasons and not out of a sense of entitlement, which means you must resist the temptation to take shortcuts and skip steps.

No one is entitled to or "due" anything in their professional lives. Everyone must pay their dues, which includes following a logical progression of steps along their career path. This is especially important for leaders because you can't serve and mentor people if you haven't walked in their shoes, having gained first-hand experience performing tasks common to their job, not the least of which is addressing conflict.

Would you want to be mentored by someone who has never performed the essential duties of your job or had to work through the position-specific conflicts? At a minimum, leaders should be able to ask their mentors this simple question: "When you were in my position, how did you do this?"

[handwritten margin note: Democratic Strategic Transformational Leader]

What Is Your Leadership Philosophy?

While it's important to understand your professional mission that incorporates and acknowledges your strengths, your passion, and how you can use those to serve others, it's also important to spend time thinking about your leadership philosophy.

If you don't know what you truly believe about leadership and are unable to clearly articulate it for yourself and others, it will be very difficult to be an effective and happy leader. While this may not be apparent on the good days, it will become painfully obvious on the bad days when you're confronted with difficult decisions and, like most people under pressure, regress to your default settings.

[handwritten margin note: Understand, Monitor Navigate - Build Goal - Vision oriented]

Are You Ready to Learn?

Finally, going into a new leadership position and starting over, especially in higher education, requires a willingness to learn and be teachable. Are you willing to spend time, almost daily, learning about leadership, your new area of expertise? Are you willing to read books, listen to podcasts, network with other leaders, and seek out their advice? Approach learning about leadership as if you were preparing to teach a new course or earning an additional degree. The best way to improve an organization is to improve the leader. Therefore, when you improve yourself, you are also improving those you serve.

[handwritten margin note: Improve Problem Solve What's Best for Students/Faculty SAO]

In the end, leading an academic department as the chair can be a very rewarding and fulfilling experience if you do so for the right reasons and are willing to learn, which oftentimes means teaching yourself and, most importantly, being humble enough to learn from others.

Are you ready to lead? The remainder of this book will hopefully challenge you to better identify and reflect upon your true intentions for seeking the chair position, including how to better understand yourself and others, how to build an effective culture, how to address conflict and lead in times of crisis, how to hire great people, how to serve students, and how to know if and when it's time to leave the chair position for other opportunities.

Chapter 2

People Are Your Business

- Honing the Hatchet will not delay woodcutting
- You can't go back and change the beginning, but you can Start from here to change the ending.
C.S. Lewis

> You don't build a business. You build people and then people build the business.
>
> —Zig Ziglar

As discussed in the previous chapter, many of the skills and accolades you acquired as a successful tenure-track faculty member will not, by themselves, make you a successful chair. However, as soon as you become a department chair, your new expertise and area of emphasis involve people. Yes, you must also be a student of leadership but, quite frankly, leadership, or at least effective leadership, requires influencing people. Therefore, you're in the "people business" now.

WELCOME TO THE "PEOPLE BUSINESS"

Relationships

As a department chair, what does it mean to be in the people business? You may think that most individuals in higher education are academics and not necessarily business people, at least not in the traditional sense of the word. However, a business could be loosely defined as a set of transactions designed to earn a monetary return. This definition also applies to your role as the chair because you must focus on transactions with those you serve in order to develop a return that is more valuable than money: healthy relationships.

You don't have to be a banker or stock broker to realize that, as a leader, your Return on Investment (ROI) will always be human capital in the form of relationships. More specifically, each time you interact with another person, a transaction occurs in which you either gain or lose equity. This is especially important for new leaders since you start with an empty account. While it might not seem significant, there will be a time in which you have to go to the people in your department and take out a loan, borrowing against some of the personal and relational equity you previously established.

In higher education, examples of "taking out a loan" with those in your department include telling others they must serve on a time-intensive committee, breaking the news that you have to change their schedule to include an early morning class, partially denying a funding request to present at an international conference or even deliver the disappointing news that they must give up their office with a window. You can come up with more examples from your own experiences in higher education but, overall, you can see the value of establishing equity through genuine relationships.

Any great salesperson knows that one of the first things you must do to be successful is to know your product. As a leader, people are your product. Reflect upon areas in which you are naturally intuitive about people and relationships and areas in which you struggle. Some people are just more gifted when it comes to interpreting human behavior, especially nonverbal cues and emotions. If this is your strength, utilize it. If not, take steps to learn more so you can at least be cognizant of the fact that there is usually more than meets the eye when interpreting human behavior and emotions.

Additionally, take time to step back and observe others individually as well as in small- and large-group settings. Pay attention to the dynamics of those in your department, keeping in mind that still waters run deep so the loudest, most outgoing, and outspoken person might not necessarily be the deepest thinker or even the consensual voice of reason within the department. Observe people in your department in informal situations, such as before a meeting starts. Do they talk, laugh, and appear to enjoy each other's company or do they sit quietly and choose not to engage with one another?

To further support your efforts to better understand your people, recognize that it's your job to work with and serve everyone. Similar to how a mayor of a city can't decide which citizens or part of the town they will serve, you show up every day to be everyone's leader, which means accepting them completely as they are. To modify a commonly used phrase in public education of "every student, every day," your daily mantra should be "every person, every day." To further illustrate this, look at the following statements and think about the many ways these could be completed:

- At times, people are or can be_____ (positive and negative characteristics).
- At times, people are not or can't be_____ (positive and negative characteristics).

For example, one could say, "At times, people can be irrational, happy, sad, unpredictable, mean, greedy, etc." The point of forcing yourself to complete this activity, which is most effective if first written and then read out loud, is that it's a clear reminder that most of these sentences, at times, can also be true of you. Therefore, be mindful of the various seasons or moods that people encounter and offer them the benefit of the doubt.

It's also helpful to remind yourself that being in the people business means serving everyone, every day, which includes working with those who might trigger negative emotions. Therefore, complete the following sentences to identify personal biases that could unintentionally cause you to treat others differently.

- I am easily irritated by people who_____.
- I prefer not to work with people who_____.
- In my personal and professional life, the people with whom I have had the most problems, friction or arguments are_____.

After finishing these statements with descriptions and actions that relate to the types of people that upset you or have been some of your least-favorite people, complete the following, making sure to say it out loud:

- As a leader, it is my duty to work with, serve, love and mentor those who are_____. (complete with the various descriptions and actions from above).

It's alright if you need to take a minute to process this. Leadership isn't showing up to only make the easy decisions and it certainly doesn't mean you can only serve the people you like or those who make you happy and will always agree with you. How is this possible? What's the secret? Love.

Leadership isn't showing up to only make the easy decisions and it certainly doesn't mean you can only serve the people you like or those who make you happy and will always agree with you.

Leading with Love

While it's important for leaders to understand people, to reach your potential as a leader, and to help those you serve be successful, you must develop authentic relationships, which can only occur if you love them—especially, if you don't particularly like them. You may be thinking, "What? Love the people I work with, including those I don't like? Wait a minute, this is higher education and we have a human resources officer who always talks about inappropriate relationships, harassment and Title IX. Are you kidding me?"

No, this is not a joke. As a leader, you must first know your people or "know 'em to grow 'em" and this can only be accomplished if you lead with love. As Clay Scroggins says in his book *How to Lead When You're Not in Charge*, "Loving someone and leading them are a package deal. You can't have one without the other."[1]

Among the multiple definitions of "Love" that can be found in the dictionary, only a few refer to an intimate or physical relationship between two people. The majority of definitions use words and phrases such as kinship, affection, attachment, admiration, common interests, devotion, enthusiasm, loyal concern, and value.[2] In fact, in their book *The 5 Languages of Appreciation in the Workplace: Empowering Organizations by Encouraging People*, Gary Chapman and Paul White talk about how to recognize and implement the following love or appreciation languages in a professional setting:[3]

1. Words of Affirmation
   • The use of written and/or oral language (publicly and/or privately) to value the work and contribution of others.
2. Quality Time
   • Spending time with others, in work-appropriate settings, to show value through listening and shared experiences.
3. Acts of Service
   • Helping a colleague to review their work, finish a project or write a letter of recommendation for them.
4. Tangible Gifts
   • Providing small, work-appropriate gifts to value others contributions. This could be as simple as a hand-written note or a gift certificate to purchase a cup of coffee or snack.
5. Physical Touch
   • This is obviously work appropriate and consists of showing others value through a congratulatory handshake, high five, fist bump, or pat on the back. However, please be respectful of others and always ask them permission before you engage in any type of physical contact in the workplace. For example, "Congratulations on your promotion, may I pat you on the back?"

As you can see, love is a verb which means it's an act that you show or do for others, and comes in many varieties. The old adage of "people don't care how much you know until they know how much you care" is very appropriate here. To lead is to build relationships and authentic relationships can only be built upon a loving foundation. In short, "you gotta love 'em to lead 'em."

As the leader of your department, leading with love doesn't mean you will always like people and they will always like you. It also doesn't mean that, as the chair, you are a pushover and everyone gets their way and no one's feelings are ever hurt. That's not realistic. For example, think about your personal relationships with friends, relatives, significant others, or, perhaps, your own children. Without a doubt, there are times that even though you still love them (i.e., are concerned about them, care about them, have a kinship with them), you may really dislike them. Nonetheless, you still treat them in a way that is respectful, is mindful of their feelings and communicates that while you may be temporarily disappointed or upset with their behavior, you still care about them and want what's best.

In all honesty, you will be asked to lead, serve, and mentor people with whom you have very little in common or whom you simply do not like. You will lead people who, for no apparent or justifiable reason, do not like you. It doesn't matter. You're the leader. Be the bigger person and relentlessly lead them with love. You don't have to like them but you must, at all times, keep in mind that they are human, have feelings, and should be treated accordingly. This isn't easy but if it were, anyone could do the job. Remember, "every person, every day."

As a final reminder of the importance of leading with love, consider the following acronym:

- **L**ead
- **O**thers with
- **V**ulnerability and
- **E**mpathy

DEVELOPING RELATIONSHIPS

As an imperfect person leading other imperfect people, some of whom you won't like and/or won't like you, it's now clear that you must work to lead with love and develop relationships. While there will always be a certain distance you keep from others, which is also buffered by the formalities of the workplace, the following suggestions are nonetheless sincere and not merely a checklist of things to do to show you are trying to develop relationships.

In their book *In Search of Excellence: Lessons from America's Best-Run Companies*,[4] Tom Peters and Robert Waterman presented the notion of "Management by Walking Around." Considered innovative at the time, this essentially encouraged managers or leaders to get to know the people in their organizations through being more visible and engaging in informal conversations to ultimately develop stronger relationships. As the name implies, this encouraged leaders to leave their somewhat isolated offices and board rooms to literally "walk around" and get to know people.

As a department chair, it's important that you are visible to all of your stakeholders, especially faculty, staff, and students. While it's easy to give into the temptation of sending one more email or making one more phone call, similar to developing any other discipline, make it a point to schedule and complete your "rounds" every day. The informal conversations you have with others, typically while standing in the hall or doorway of their office, are a key ingredient to developing relationships and building relational equity.

The following is a list of questions and suggestions to help you better understand yourself and how to build relationships with others:

- How do you typically interact with others? Are you a good listener? Do you maintain eye contact? Do you interrupt? Ask a trusted friend or colleague to analyze how you communicate and share any behaviors that might, unintentionally, be perceived as rude or aloof.
- How do you prefer to have your leaders communicate and build relationships with you? Keep in mind that your preferred method might not work with everyone else.
- How do you typically build relationships with others (personally and professionally)? Are relationships easy or difficult for you?
- Do your relationships have a positive or negative pattern? If so, be aware that this may affect how you build professional relationships.
- Schedule time each day to get up, walk around, and talk to people. Just like a doctor in a hospital, do your rounds, and take care of people.
- Take time to quickly jot down or journal your interactions for follow up. For example, if someone mentions their child has an important soccer game that evening, make it a point to ask them the outcome the next time you chat. Also, pay close attention to the professional goals of those in your department so you can share future opportunities with them. Remember, you must "know 'em to grow 'em".
- Be willing to be wrong and admit it. This isn't to say you must spill your life secrets and cross personal boundaries but the truth is, you will never be perfect so embrace it and admit it. This also includes a willingness to sincerely apologize when you make mistakes, which is yet another way to build relational equity with others.
- Keep in mind that you are always the chair or leader of the department which means you are always "on," representing all stakeholders, especially students. Therefore, anytime you are "walking around" you are leading and

setting an example. This is equally important when you are on campus and out in the community.

We Bring Ourselves to Work Each Day

In addition to being mindful of the importance of building relationships, identifying your personal triggers or characteristics that you would naturally prefer not to work with and always trying to lead with love, it's important to dig a bit deeper and realize that the one thing we always bring to work is ourselves.

Please know that what follows is not meant to serve as professional counseling advice or be upsetting or demeaning. As a leader, it's important to realize that people are human and despite their best intentions and efforts, the "stuff" or baggage that everyone carries around and tries to deal with will also come to work and affect their behavior, performance, and interactions with others. While it's not your job to fix people (leave that to the trained professionals), it will help you to better understand and be more compassionate and empathetic toward those you serve.

The impact of trauma on public school children has received a considerable amount of attention over the past decade. According to Jessica Minahan, a licensed, board-certified behavior analyst, "Up to two-thirds of U.S. children have experienced at least one type of serious childhood trauma, such as abuse, neglect, natural disaster or experience witnessing violence."[5] According to the Center for Disease Control and Prevention, traumatic events that occur in childhood (up to the age of seventeen) contribute to Adverse Childhood Experiences or ACEs. Among adults surveyed across twenty-five states, 61 percent reported experiencing at least one adverse experience; almost 16 percent indicated they had experienced four or more.[6]

Examples of ACEs include:

- Emotional, physical, and/or sexual abuse
- Emotional and/or physical neglect
- Witnessing domestic violence
- Living in a household with alcoholism and/or substance abuse
- Parent separation or divorce
- Exposure to suicide attempts or a death by suicide

Unfortunately, the effects of childhood trauma and adverse experiences can continue to have a negative impact throughout one's life. In fact, people with four or more ACEs are more susceptible to health risks such as alcoholism, drug abuse, depression, and suicide attempts.[7] In addition, the International Society for Traumatic Stress Studies reports that adults who experienced childhood trauma can struggle with feelings of anxiety, guilt, shame, and anger, in addition to having problems developing authentic relationships with others.[8]

Within the context of understanding others and building relationships as a leader, the goal of understanding childhood trauma and ACEs is to serve as a gentle reminder that everyone is human, life isn't always easy or fair and despite their best efforts, there are some things that people have endured or witnessed years ago that stick with them, causing them to behave and interact in ways they may not be aware of. As a result, people can carry these experiences and associated behaviors everywhere they go, including the workplace.

As an effective leader, especially in times of conflict and crisis, be mindful of the fact that everyone has gone through or is currently experiencing a difficult time and may behave or react in ways that have very little to do with you or the organization. If you want to be angry or frustrated with someone, ask them their problems. If you want to be compassionate, caring, and helpful, find out why. As a department chair, if you or one of your colleagues is suffering from any type of depression, trauma, or mental anguish, please seek professional assistance.

Hopefully, you now have a better understanding and appreciation for what it means to be in the people business. All organizations, regardless of their successes or failures, are comprised of people who are all perfectly imperfect. As the department chair, as your relationship with your people goes, so goes the success of the department. Granted, you might not like everyone and they may not like you, but you still need to know your people, build relationships, and always lead with love. Remember, people are now your business.

Chapter 3

It's Not All about You

Leadership is a choice, not a position.
—Stephen Covey

According to Simon Sinek, "How a leader lists their priorities reveals their bias. And their bias will influence the choices they make."[1] Before becoming a department chair, you most likely developed an established daily agenda, guided by your priority or bias to achieve tenure and/or promotion, thus focusing on your teaching, research, and service. The life of a tenure-track university professor, while demanding, does offer some flexibility. For example, you can frequently choose where you work on your research or prepare for classes. It was neither a requirement nor an expectation that you clocked into the office Monday through Friday from 9 a.m. to 5 p.m., twelve months out of the year.

In addition, while you obviously had to be mindful of your colleagues and students, it's doubtful that you showed up to the office each day, primarily thinking about other people's problems and conflicts that you would have to address. Similar to a musician in an orchestra, although you had to work hard, get along well with others and be mindful of how your individual talents contributed to the overall ensemble, you were not the conductor, in charge of and constantly thinking about a myriad of variables, all of which can make or break the overall success of the group.

In his book *Leadershift: The 11 Essential Changes Every Leader Must Embrace*, the first change that John Maxwell presents is the "Focus Shift," which he also compares to going from the role of a soloist to the conductor, saying, "you can be a successful person on your own, but not a successful leader."[2] Similarly, while faculty members must collaborate with their colleagues and are accountable for their individual contributions to the group,

21

it's not their job to be responsible for the group. As the leader of the department, your daily priority or bias is to be responsible for the individuals
within the department, which means putting them first and realizing it's not
all about you.

YOUR DAILY AGENDA

The change in priorities and daily commitments are perhaps some of the
more surprising and difficult adjustments for chairs to make. Not only are you
expected to be on campus more often, maybe twelve months out of the year,
but you will have many more meetings than you had as a professor. Some
days it will seem like all you do is go from one meeting to the next. The transition from faculty member to department chair can be a significant change to
your daily agenda. To be clear, daily means each and every day. What you do
on a daily basis matters, and will be guided and informed by your leadership
philosophy and priorities.

Which Self Are You Serving Today?

Each day as you prepare to go into the office and consider your daily agenda,
be aware of which "self" you are serving. Have you been selfish and prioritized yourself over others or are you selfless, committed to serving others?
As soon as you accept any leadership position, especially in higher education, you are not the most important person on your agenda. In fact, you are
not entirely in control of your daily agenda. Remember, you're in the people
business now which means you show up each day, literally and figuratively
to serve others.

> What you do on a daily basis matters, and will be guided and informed by
> your leadership philosophy and priorities.

As you consider your agenda and establish a selfless, servant-based mindset, realize that throughout the day, you are like a physician who is constantly
diagnosing symptoms (problems) and prescribing appropriate treatments
(solutions). In addition, similar to how a physician doesn't avoid the hospital
because it's full of sick people, leaders approach each day with the mindset
and understanding that they are walking toward the problems and conflicts
because it's part of the job.

From a leadership perspective, what types of problems are you drawn to and like to solve? Are you passionate about solving "people" problems on a daily basis among faculty, staff, students, and other stakeholders? Although it is neither natural nor expected to be completely comfortable with the uncomfortable from the first day, assessing the extent to which you actually enjoy and are intuitive about solving people problems can be a strong indicator of your ability to not only survive but, more importantly, thrive as a department chair.

POWERFUL QUESTIONS TO GUIDE THE DAY

In addition to being mindful of the compounding impact of each day, primarily guided by your daily agenda, it's also important to recognize that leadership is challenging because no one is perfect, including you. Accordingly, you will experience days when you would much rather serve yourself by hiding in your office (or at home) and not worrying about other people. Although these days should be the exception, there are definitely days where you best serve others by serving (i.e., taking care of) yourself and taking a day off. Therefore, try to start each day with powerful and critical questions that can establish a positive, servant-based mindset.

In *Dream Like a Champion: Wins, Losses, and Leadership the Nebraska Volleyball Way*, John Cook, one of the most successful collegiate volleyball coaches in history (four national championships; thirteen conference championships), asks himself the following three questions each day:[3]

1. Who needs me today?
2. Would I be chosen again for this job?
3. Would I want to be coached by me?

A modified and extended version for department chairs is to start each day with the following questions:

- Who needs me today?
- Would I be hired again?
- Would I want to be my chair or leader today?
- Am I willing to be uncomfortable for others?
- Does my attitude and agenda say "I deserve" or "I'm here to serve"?

Who Needs Me Today?

This is perhaps the most powerful, daily question any leader can ask themselves and directly establishes a selfless attitude. While there are many people you serve and need to be mindful of on a daily basis, there are some that will need you more than others and for different reasons. For example, one person might need a simple word or note of encouragement, while someone else may need an in-depth conversation. In addition, the person who needs you may not actually need you to solve anything but merely listen and validate their concerns. No matter the situation, you're in the people business, which means people will need you every day.

Would I be Hired Again?

This question is very powerful because it helps maintain an adequate level of creative tension, which can keep leaders current, relevant, and humble. The question is also beneficial for the job market. For example, it's not enough to question if you would be hired again for your current position but, more importantly, would you be hired for a similar position at a peer institution or one that would represent an advancement? Overall, ask yourself if you're working and planning each day to remain relevant and competitive on the job market, which ultimately makes you a better leader for your current department.

Would I Want to Be My Chair or Leader Today?

Regardless of one's profession, this is a powerful question because it forces people to step back and observe themselves and how they affect others. When you start each day, take into consideration your daily agenda along with your attitude, especially if it's not positive. Ask yourself if you would like to be your leader today? What if you were the person who needed their leader the most today, would you want your current outlook and attitude? This isn't to discount your feelings and suggest you are not entitled to less-than-stellar days, it's simply a reminder to step back and assess how your daily agenda and attitude can affect others.

Am I Willing to Be Uncomfortable for Others?

There are many ways to analyze and approach this question but, at its core, it's about courage. Are you willing to step up and be the chair your department needs by being uncomfortable? As Brené Brown suggests, are you willing to choose "courage over comfort?"[4] Serving others isn't easy and great leaders are always courageous. Remember, similar to a firefighter running into a burning building, your daily agenda will require you to show courage and step into uncomfortable situations to best serve others.

"I Deserve" vs. "I'm Here to Serve"

As a leader, are you showing up with a selfish attitude of "I deserve" or a servant-based mindset of "I'm here to serve"? This is an important question because it's only natural, as a human being, to have days where you would rather be a bit more selfish. It's natural to become stressed or discouraged and adopt a sense of entitlement, focusing on what you deserve. When it comes to serving others, you may oftentimes feel as though you are giving more than you are receiving, which will probably be true. Nonetheless, be mindful of falling into a negative attitude of focusing only on what you deserve, forgetting that it's your job to serve.

As a department chair, how you plan, perceive, and carry out each day will ultimately contribute to the sum of who you are as a leader and what you can accomplish as a department. Although no one is perfect and everyone experiences good days and bad days, taking the time to ask yourself the aforementioned questions can help you establish a positive attitude and be the leader your people and organization need each and every day.

> How you plan, perceive, and carry out each day will ultimately contribute to the sum of who you are as a leader and what you can accomplish as a department.

HOW TO LEAD YOUR DAILY AGENDA

Even though your daily agenda and commitments, especially compared to your pre-chair life, are often out of your control, realize that you are still in control. In fact, despite giving up much of your time to others, it's important to take time for yourself, both personally and professionally. You can't do your job and serve others if you're always running on empty.

In his bestselling book *The 7 Habits of Highly Effective People*, Stephen Covey's seventh habit, "Sharpen the Saw," is also the most important because he says that "it is the habit that makes all the others possible."[5] Covey goes on to state that we must take time to sharpen our saw by focusing on the Four Dimensions of Renewal:[6]

1. Physical (exercise, nutrition, stress management).
2. Mental (reading, visualizing, planning, writing).
3. Social/Emotional (service, empathy, synergy, intrinsic security).
4. Spiritual (value clarification and commitment, study and meditation).

Covey's 7 Habits should be required reading for all leaders but for the sake of brevity, the best way to sharpen the saw and take time for yourself daily is to be purposeful and schedule it.

Schedule Yourself

Since most of our lives are driven by our daily agenda, the first place to start is your calendar. From a professional standpoint, even though an administrative assistant may have access to your calendar and the ability to schedule appointments without your consent, you can still carve out time for yourself within the workday. Granted, there will always be standing meetings that occur at scheduled times as well as things that unexpectedly come up. However, since you regularly attend the standing meetings that you don't control, schedule and attend meetings with yourself that you do control.

For example, if it's important to exercise during the week, block it off in your calendar. If you need to make time for your research, make it a standing, scheduled appointment. Even though serving others as their chair can be demanding, you have to take time for yourself by making it a part of your daily agenda.

Finally, make sure that your administrative assistant and staff are aware of your desire to guard your personal time. The value of a great administrative assistant could be a book by itself. Oftentimes, your assistant serves as your "first line of defense" in terms of scheduling and protecting your time so make sure they are aware and will also help to hold you accountable to keeping the appointments you have with yourself.

Delegate

As a department chair, you cannot, nor should you be expected to do it all. In fact, because you are in a university, you are surrounded by very intelligent people with advanced degrees who are capable of doing things that enhance the department. Make it a point to identify people who have talents in areas in which you are weak and empower them to act. Delegating certain responsibilities does not mean you are neglecting your duties but rather, it is a way to develop and mentor your colleagues.

Have a Mentor

In addition to mentoring others, it's important that you continue to have at least one mentor who can speak into your life and provide motivation or simply listen when you need to vent. Due to the hectic nature of your schedule and the inherent frustration and stress it may cause, working with a mentor is also a form of self-care and making time for yourself. Keep in mind that a true mentoring relationship doesn't happen overnight. It takes time to develop a relationship with someone and must be mutually beneficial; you should also be able to help the other person. Overall, you must be willing to hear and share the truth, which can be uncomfortable but is always necessary for growth.

YOUR PERSONAL LIFE ISN'T PERSONAL

As a department chair, you must show up each day with a selfless attitude, willing to serve others, which has a significant impact on your daily agenda. However, there isn't a chair hat you put on in the morning upon arriving to the office and then hang up at the end of the day when you leave. You are *always* the chair, which is the public face and representative of your department. Always means always, including when you are at the grocery store, stuck in traffic, at your kid's dance recital, or, most importantly, posting to social media. Like it or not, you are a 24/7 walking, talking billboard for your department, college, university, and stakeholders.

You might be thinking to yourself that you are entitled to a private, personal life and can't be expected to work 24 hours a day, 365 days out of the year. You're correct. There isn't a human resources department in the United States that would force you to work nonstop. However, even though you are not always "on the clock," you are always "on the stage" and this should not be taken lightly.

> You are *always* the chair, which is the public face and representative of your department.

Visible and Attractive

To be up-front and honest, it probably isn't fair that, whether you want them to or not, people will likely associate your actions, thoughts, and social media posts with those of the department, college, and/or university. However, this is the reality of the world you live in. In fact, it has a name—cancel culture— which is a form of "cancelling" or ostracizing almost everything associated with a person or group due to their professed actions and/or beliefs, albeit personal or professional. While cancel culture may be commonly associated with celebrities, it can affect almost any person and organization.

As the leader of your department, you are highly visible and very attractive—everyone sees you and your behavior attracts attention. Stakeholders, such as students, community members, and colleagues, see you and are attracted to the position you hold and what it represents. As a result, people could take offense to something you say or do, directly attribute it to your position as chair and essentially "cancel" their association with your department, college, and/or university. Consider the following scenario:

> At the beginning of the current academic year, Dr. Newchair started his job as a department chair at Local State University. At his previous institution, Dr. Newchair was a dynamic teacher and scholar, known for his firm political views, which he would frequently share in class, in the community and especially on social media. While people may not have always agreed with Dr. Newchair's points of view, most would agree that he was a nice person.

> Upon assuming his role as a first-year department chair, Dr. Newchair continued to share his opinions, especially on social media, which included his frustration with the local city council in which he called for the mayor's resignation. His behavior and opinions soon caught the attention of faculty and students within his department as well as alumni and stakeholders associated with the university. Furthermore, one of the mayor's closest business associates happened to be a prominent donor to the college in which Dr. Newchair's department was located and promptly expressed his concern to the university President.

In analyzing this scenario, you may think that Dr. Newchair is entitled to his opinions, which is true. In addition, you might dig a little deeper and conclude that while it's not advisable for a department chair to call for the mayor's resignation, Dr. Newchair certainly didn't do so in a way that was illegal or even threatening, which is also true. In fact, one could say that as a member of a university that promotes diversity, equity, and inclusion and encourages students and faculty to express their views, Dr. Newchair is setting an example, which could also be true. So then, what's the problem in this scenario? The issue is that whether he realizes it or not, Dr. Newchair's views and choice of language could be construed as representative of his entire department, college, and/or university.

Again, you may be thinking, "This isn't fair. People are entitled to their thoughts, opinions and private lives." To some extent, yes, but the bigger issue to consider is that nobody forced Dr. Newchair to become the leader of this department. As an educated adult, he freely accepted the position and responsibility. Furthermore, in higher education, people receive promotion and tenure tied to a faculty position, regardless of if they serve an administrative role. Therefore, those who decide to assume the awesome responsibility of leading an academic department must be willing to make both professional and personal sacrifices.

QUESTIONS TO CONSIDER

According to Michael Fraccaro, chief human resources officer for the credit card company Mastercard, "Your leaders are the megaphone for the company's culture. In a world of sound bites and tweets, our leaders have a moral obligation in what they say and how they behave."[7] Whether it's fair or not, as the leader of your department, you are always speaking through the megaphone, representing a large, diverse number of stakeholders such as students, parents, your bosses, faculty, staff, alumni, and donors. Therefore, consider the following questions before you speak or act out publicly.

Does This Represent All Stakeholders?

As the full-time billboard for your department, almost everything you say and do in a public setting or forum is fair game to be scrutinized and associated with your department. People could assume that your thoughts represent those of the department and related stakeholders. Therefore, ask yourself if what you are about to communicate adequately represents and reflects each and every one of the aforementioned people. In addition, would you be comfortable sharing this message face-to-face, one-on-one, with each of these people? If the answer is "no," or you are not sure, then don't say it or do it.

Does This Align with the Mission and Values?

This may seem like a lot to ask but it's appropriate, especially within the context of cancel culture. As a chair, your words and actions are connected to your department, college, and university. Therefore, before you act or speak publically, ask yourself if it's in line with the mission and values of everyone associated with your department, college, and university. Again, would you go in front of each of these people, including the dean, provost, and president, and act this way or make these comments to their face? Furthermore, what does this say about you and your character, both personally and professionally?

Remember, when it comes to leadership or positions of perceived importance, most people want to be but fewer want to do. In addition, the sacrifices and trade-offs aren't a one-time decision or event but something you do each and every day. The personal and professional things you can do and say on a daily basis as a department chair are not the same as when you were a professor.

In the end, making the decision to serve others, in any capacity, is making the decision to forego being the most important person on your daily agenda. In addition, the reason there are more workers than leaders in the world is that most people have to work to earn a living, but leaders choose to make the service of others their work. Therefore, as a leader, you must give up certain rights, privileges, and preferences, both personally and professionally, because it's no longer all about you.

Chapter 4

Leadership Requires Courage

People don't follow titles. They follow courage.
—William Wells Brown

According to Brené Brown, a leader is "anyone who takes responsibility for finding the potential in people and processes, and who has the courage to develop that potential."[1] She goes on to state that "we desperately need more leaders who are committed to courageous, wholehearted leadership and who are self-aware enough to lead from their hearts, rather than unevolved leaders who lead from hurt and fear."[2] Those who lead from hurt and fear do so in hopes of appearing competent and in control. However, the best leaders are those who are willing to embrace their vulnerability by admitting their flaws and fears. Simply stated, leadership takes courage.

LEADERSHIP REQUIRES COURAGE

Leadership is influence through character, courage, relationships, and service. Leaders who lack courage, fail to build authentic relationships, and don't put others first may eventually create unhealthy organizations, the consequences of which can be low morale and high turnover. For example, consider the five most common traits of a bad boss that emerged after surveying over 1,000 people:[3]

1. Rude and disrespectful treatment of others
2. Criticizing people in front of their peers
3. Systematically turning down ideas and initiatives
4. Always having a "been-there, done-that" attitude
5. Lying to people at work

Obviously, these are not the actions of an effective leader who is in the position for the right reasons. In addition, these are not reflective of a leader who is willing to be vulnerable and make mistakes. As a result, it's easy to see how bad leaders can create unhappy people which ultimately leads to an unhappy organization.

> Leadership is influence through character, courage, relationships, and service.

John Grogan, author of the book *Marley and Me: Life and Love with the World's Worst Dog*, which was later made into a popular movie, said, "There's no such thing s a bad dog, just a bad owner."[4] The same could be said about leaders and organizations: There are no bad organizations, just bad leaders. Great leadership requires great courage.

Since leadership is always the one thing that can change everything, it's easy to see the transformational benefits of leading with courage, which can change people's morale, work ethic, and overall level of happiness and fulfillment. Better leaders create happier, more productive people who ultimately create a better organization.

BEING A COURAGEOUS CHAIR

As the chair of your department, each day you will have the opportunity, decision by decision, to do the right thing, and lead with courage. Granted, it's not easy but if it were, anyone could be an effective leader. Also, keep in mind that every decision and action, or lack thereof, sends a message, which means your silence can sometimes be the loudest message of all. Just like you are *always* the chair and representative of your department, you are *always* making decisions and sending messages whether you speak or not.

As a department chair, being comfortable with the uncomfortable also means being comfortable with the fact that those who love you today may loathe you tomorrow, and vice versa. Honestly, it's only natural to want to be liked because it simply feels better and reduces anxiety and negative thoughts and emotions. However, unlike your pre-chair days when you had to be mindful of whom you might offend in case they were on your promotion and tenure committee, as a chair, you must be OK with not being OK.

While it's always necessary to look at the big picture and be considerate of others, you cannot avoid the difficult decisions simply because you're scared of what others may think. This takes courage. The following offers specific examples in the life of a department chair that require courage such as being a filter, asking courageous questions, and choosing courage daily.

Being a Filter

Academic chairs are not only the face of the department but are also the filter. Most people don't realize just how much dirt and debris the air filter in their house protects them from on a daily basis. As the chair, you serve a similar function for your department. Granted, this doesn't mean you have to physically get dirty and breathe in debris, but you are constantly serving as the first line of defense, protecting your people so they can best serve students and the university through teaching, research, and service. What follows are specific examples of how the chair serves courageously as a department filter.

Complaint Filter

You're in the people business which means you will have to deal with complaints. As the chair of your department, you will serve and answer to a number of stakeholders, all of whom may contact you with questions and/or to share less-than-positive opinions. While it's not normal to want to field complaints, which can include being treated rudely, it's now part of your job.

As a professor, you would not have been overly enthusiastic if your chair asked you to come into their office to talk to an upset student who wasn't in your class. It wasn't part of your job. However, it's now your job so think of yourself as the chief complaint officer. It may not be pleasant but keep in mind that every time you courageously address a complaint, be it from a student, community member, or even a colleague within your own department, you are simultaneously sending a message to those in your department that you care about them and are willing to protect their time so they can do their job.

Conflict Filter

Yes, you will deal with a lot of conflict as a chair and it will come in many shapes, sizes, and flavors. Although subsequent chapters will cover conflict more in-depth, it's appropriate to mention here that much of the conflict you address requires you to serve as a filter. For example, even the best families, organizations, and academic departments have arguments, drama, and old-fashioned "people problems." The good news is that many of these problems tend to be the result of either poor communication (i.e., a misunderstanding) or unmet, unrealistic expectations. Nonetheless, it's your job to stand at the front of the line, approach the conflict head-on, and serve as the filter, which ultimately serves others.

Administrative Filter

As a department chair, you are the epitome of middle management. This means you are a two-way filter, caught between (1) your department, which represents the faculty, and (2) your dean, who advocates for and answers to the administration. At times, this means going to the dean, your boss, and wearing your professor hat in support and advocacy of the department. Other times, you have to put on your administrator hat and go to your department in support and advocacy of the dean and/or upper-level administration. This can be a difficult and delicate balancing act to figure out and, above all, requires courage.

Despite your best intentions, you are not going to get it right 100 percent of the time which means you will have uncomfortable conversations with your department and your Dean. However, this doesn't mean that you are a bad person or a bad leader as long as you still approach the position for the right reasons and conduct yourself with integrity. Overall, it's your job to be this conduit or filter, serving both sides of the academic/administrative fence.

An important note to consider within the context of serving as the administrative filter is that your Dean also wears multiple hats, serving as a filter between their various chairs and departments and the university's upper administration. Therefore, be mindful of the fact that those to whom you report also have different strengths and weaknesses and should be afforded the benefit of the doubt, the same as your faculty will certainly have to give to you. Having the courage to serve as the administrative filter means you must be willing to treat and, at times, lead your boss with the same level of compassion, understanding, and grace with which you treat those in your department.

If serving as a filter seems lonely and you wish others would understand just how much you do to serve and protect them (i.e., filter out debris), then you're doing it right. Not only does it take courage to constantly stand in the busy intersection of faculty, administration, and stakeholders, it's a critical part of the chair position. In fact, a quick Google search related to the difficulties or thankless aspects of serving as a department chair will reveal that it is one of the most challenging leadership roles on most university campuses. In *The Essential Department Chair: A Comprehensive Desk Reference*, Jeffery Buller eloquently captures the magnitude and scope of the chair position saying, "The job of chairing a department is probably the most important, least appreciated, and toughest administrative position in higher education."[5]

Courageous Questions

You will have to show up and be courageous on a daily basis and while this may never be completely comfortable, it's possible to improve in this area. Asking questions is an effective way to learn and to grow; leaders must be willing to hear what they fear by asking courageous questions. Consider the following questions which can be used to build relationships and lead with courage.

Leaders must be willing to hear what they fear by asking courageous questions.

What Do I Need to Know or Hear?

This may seem rather benign at first but asking your faculty, staff, colleagues, stakeholders, and supervisors this question is giving them permission to be honest, knowing it might not be pleasant or comfortable for either of you. A more direct way of asking this question is to say, "Tell me what I don't want to hear." As a chair, you are making yourself vulnerable by asking this question and while it might seem odd, in doing so, you are showing courage and building relational equity with others. Almost everyone in higher education has an opinion and although it might not be comfortable at first, offering people an open door to be honest is the sign of an effective leader.

Other variations of this question which you can choose, based upon the situation, are as follows:

- How do you feel about this?
- Is there something you would like to say but haven't?
- What am I missing?
- If forced to share one concern or complaint about this, what would it be?
- Where have I failed to meet your expectations?
- What will I probably miss or not understand?

Do You Have Everything You Need?

This is a very vague question and could be asked in a number of contexts with a multitude of responses, which is why it's powerful and courageous. Also, the implication is that you want to make sure people have everything they need to be successful. At its most basic level, this can be your "go to" question when doing your daily rounds and informally checking in on people because it shows concern while also extending an invitation to communicate with you.

For example, it's the beginning of the fall semester and you pop into Dr. S's office and ask if he has everything he needs. His response could range from "Yes, I'm doing fine. Thanks for asking" to "No. I thought my supplies would be here by now and I'm beginning to panic." Granted, there are many places and reasons to ask this question and the responses can vary but, overall, it shows your concern and willingness to help, if necessary.

What Do You Have?

Again, this is an open-ended question, has many applications and can be asked multiple times in a day, thus making it effective. And yes, it takes courage to ask this question because the responses and related discussions can go in a thousand directions.

This question is probably most used when a faculty member comes into your office with an unannounced or unscheduled question, comment or concern. For example, you're sitting at your desk with your office door open and Dr. X asks if you have a few minutes. After greeting her appropriately and a little small talk, you ask her, "What do you have?" It might seem rather simple but it's very powerful as it not only moves the conversation forward but also implies that you really want to know what she "has" and can do for her.

In fact, T. Boone Pickens, a well-known oil magnate and multimillionaire, claimed that his version of this question *Whaddya got* was not only his most important but was also how he "jump-started" each meeting as it would set the tone and hold people accountable for coming prepared.[6]

What's the One Thing That Could Change Everything?

Based on the concept that "leadership is the one thing that can change everything," asking individuals or groups what's the "one thing that could change everything" is very effective. This question is especially powerful in its ability to cause people to direct their focus on the most important variable. Using this question also requires courage (i.e., vulnerability) because you never know what the other person might say and where that might lead the conversation.

For example, Dr. B., a professor in your department, comes to you very frustrated with his upcoming schedule, claiming that it doesn't leave him enough time for research. One way to potentially get to the root of his concern and/or the problem would be to say the following: "Dr. B., I understand your frustration and want to help. If we both had a magic wand and could fix this, what's the one thing that would change everything?" One noteworthy caveat to this question that may sound humorous but is very helpful is that the "one thing" that could fix everything cannot (1) break any local, state, or federal laws and/or violate any university policy and (2) cannot include miracles. And while it may sound ridiculous, it is helpful to let people know these two caveats when posing the question.

Are We Doing This for the Right Reasons?

Regardless of the scenario or context, actions, timing, and reasons should always be considered. Ask yourself if you are making the right decision at the right time for the right reasons. Like all courageous questions, this has multiple applications. Asking this question also ensures that your decisions are in line with the mission, purpose, and strategic plan of the department, college, and university.

For example, your department has been asked by the dean and provost to consider pursuing national accreditation related to your primary undergraduate program, which would help to better market the program and attract students. However, it will require an intensive and expensive two-year process to seek preliminary accreditation, which will reduce the amount of time some faculty have to commit to their students, research, and service obligations. Using this question would target the following variables:

- Actions—Should we consider pursuing national accreditation and why? Is it the right thing to do? By saying "yes" to this, what are we saying "no" to?
- Timing—Is this the right time? As a department, can we afford to take away time from our other commitments? Can we afford the financial costs at this time?
- Reasons—What are the reasons for this and are they valid? For example, are we a bad or inadequate program without this accreditation? Are we putting our students at a significant disadvantage for job prospects or graduate-school admission? Are the financial and personal return on investment worth it?

While this is a very basic example, it still illustrates the value of asking and breaking down the question of whether or not actions are for the right reasons and, most importantly, for the right people.

How Are You Doing?

Sometimes the simplest things can be the most effective and, at the same time, difficult to ask. While we all ask this question daily to friends, colleagues, family members, and complete strangers, the value comes through being sincere and taking time to listen to the response. Although it is certainly polite to always acknowledge people, smile, and say "Hello. How are you?" as the chair of your department, take the extra step to actually find out how people are doing. In all honesty, this might be the toughest, most courageous question because it opens the door to a number of possibilities.

In addition, the true value of this question frequently comes from asking it a second time or using another courageous question as a follow-up. For example, imagine that you are walking in the hallway outside of your office and cross paths with Dr. Q., one of your faculty members. You look her in the eye, smile, and say, "Hello, Dr. Q., how are you doing today?" She somewhat smiles, and gives a half-hearted "I'm OK." You stop walking and once again say, "How are you really doing? Do you have everything you need?"

The direction of the conversation could take a number of turns but hopefully this illustrates the power of simply taking the time to ask a rather courageous question of "How are you doing?" and not only mean it, but be willing to listen.

COMPLIMENT COURAGEOUSLY

In his book *The Infinite Game*, Simon Sinek says that "leaders are not responsible for the results, leaders are responsible for the people who are responsible for the results."[7] Although this statement can be a relief, suggesting that as the department chair you are not directly responsible for things such as faculty scholarly productivity or enrollment, it can also be rather daunting. Honestly, there are very few times in life that someone can literally force another human being to do anything. However, as the chair of the department, being responsible for the people responsible for the results (i.e., faculty and staff) ultimately has an effect on the choices and behaviors of others.

Acknowledging that you are responsible for those whom you serve and represent is a courageous decision that must be made each and every day. Success is like a sound, long-term investment that day by day earns compounding interest and, ultimately, provides a significant return. Therefore, being a courageous leader is a daily decision.

However, being responsible for others also means you must be willing to compliment and share in their success. While most of the discussion related to leading courageously has focused on either addressing conflict and how to interact with others, it's equally important to realize that as an effective chair and leader, you must be willing to acknowledge and give credit to others, which takes courage. In fact, your compliments should exponentially outnumber your critiques and conflict-related conversations. Complimenting others may seem like common sense because doing so is rarely a source of conflict and certainly makes people feel better. However, it takes courage and vulnerability to truly be happy for others' success and to recognize them appropriately.

It's neither easy nor natural to serve as a filter for complaints and conflict or to walk the fine line between your faculty and your dean. It's also difficult to be vulnerable enough to ask questions to which you don't know the answer or the potential consequences. Nonetheless, leadership requires courage and courage is a choice. Be the leader your department needs and choose courage each day.

Chapter 5

Culture Matters

Far and away the best prize that life has to offer is the chance to work hard at work worth doing.

—Teddy Roosevelt

According to Max De Pree, "The first responsibility of a leader is to define reality."[1] For better or worse, an organization's culture reflects what its people do and value on a daily basis. Therefore, as the leader of your department, part of defining reality is to recognize and understand the current culture. Culture matters and, as a leader, the moment you step into your organization you affect and are affected by its culture. Furthermore, an organization's culture is ultimately a reflection of the courage, character, and values of its leader.

THE IMPORTANCE OF ORGANIZATIONAL CULTURE

Although it is common to initially associate culture with the well-known, often-times stereotypical practices of other countries, it's important to understand the word from an organizational standpoint. Culture is defined as "the set of shared attitudes, values, goals, and practices that characterizes an institution or organization."[2] Specific to leadership, John Maxwell defines a company's culture as "the expression of the values of the people within the organization."[3]

An organization's culture is ultimately a reflection of the courage, character, and values of its leader.

An organization's culture also represents where its people live, interact, and spend a significant portion of their time. A *Glassdoor* survey found that 77 percent of adults would consider a company's culture before applying for a job.[4] This suggests that in addition to the front-facing aspects of an organization, such as what it produces and the salary and benefits, potential job applicants are concerned about the culture in which they will work and live.

Another way to think about organizational culture is like a swimming pool that everyone must swim in. Just like a pool manager, it's the leader's job to make sure the water is clean, the temperature is comfortable and, above all, the people are safe. And similar to a swimming pool, whatever gets into the water (good or bad) will ultimately affect everyone. There are no such things as "clean" and "unclean" sections of the same pool.

As the leader of your department, you are responsible for the environment that everyone lives in, which affects your ability to attract new applicants and retain current faculty and staff. The culture you create, based on who you are as a leader, will play a significant role in determining if people enjoy their jobs. In fact, a *Gallup* poll surveyed over a million people and found that among those who left their jobs voluntarily, 75 percent did so because of their manager. The full list of the predictors of turnover were as follows:[5]

1. The immediate manager
2. Poor fit for the job
3. Coworkers not committed to quality
4. Pay and benefits
5. Connection to the organization's mission and to senior management

Of these five predictors of turnover, all but one—pay and benefits—can be attributed to the organizational culture for which the leader is responsible. While "the immediate manager" is clearly related to the leader, having coworkers not committed to quality and not being connected to the organization's mission are also by-products of the leader's culture. Although pay and benefits are important, these top five predictors suggest that culture (i.e., effective leadership) accounts for the main reasons people choose to leave their jobs.

In his book *101 Tough Conversations to Have with Employees: A Manager's Guide to Addressing Performance, Conduct, and Discipline Challenges*, Paul Falcone writes,

> The difference between an active and a passive job seeker is one bad day in the office. When that proverbial straw breaks, sometimes over seemingly minor issues, the job change mechanism kicks into gear, and at best you'll have a

worker who has become mentally unemployed. Then you're faced with the "employees who quit and leave" versus the "employees who quit and stay" syndrome, and it's only a matter of time until something blows up.[6]

Some people leave their jobs because of the culture their leaders allow, enable, and ultimately create. As a department chair, you can have a profound impact on whether or not people enjoy their jobs, based on the culture of the department that you promote and permit. Furthermore, department chairs are the epitome of middle management (recall the filter analogy from a previous chapter) and middle managers "have the greatest effect on turnover out of anyone within an organization."[7]

Not to place even more pressure on you but in all honesty, as a chair, you have a tremendous opportunity to shape the culture of your department. You have the ability to create an environment in which people feel safe, feel valued, and enjoy coming to work. Leadership is the one thing that can change everything and a large part of being an effective leader is the culture you create.

CULTURE REFLECTS THE LEADER

If you want to know the values and behaviors of an organization, look at their leader. Given enough time, all organizations will reflect their leadership, both positively and negatively. Granted, microcultures can exist within any organization. For example, in higher education it's possible to have a great president and overall university culture and still have a few departments that are less-than-stellar or vice versa. However, in the end, the culture you create, intentionally or not, will largely reflect who you are as leader and can significantly affect the lives of those you serve.

Leadership Characteristics

The good news is that it's possible to identify the traits that effective leaders contribute to their cultures. For instance, Schwantes reported the top three habits found among the best managers were as follows:[8]

1. Having meaningful conversations
2. Including people in the decision-making process
3. Coaching their team

These three habits reflect the value of forming relationships, mentoring others, and putting the right people in the right positions, which enables them to be part of the decision-making process.

Google, commonly known for their "outside of the box" thinking and unconventional office spaces, also wanted to know the factors or traits that make up an effective leader. In their study, Project Oxygen, Google gathered more than 10,000 observations, surveys, and performance reviews from within their own company. The result was the *Eight Habits of Highly Effective Google Managers:*[9]

1. Be a good coach
2. Empower your team and don't micromanage
3. Express interest in employee's success and well-being
4. Be productive and result-oriented
5. Be a good communicator and listen to your team
6. Help your employees with career development
7. Have a clear vision and strategy for the team
8. Have key technical skills, so you can help advise the team

Interestingly, while technical skills made the list, it was within the context of being able to help others. Even at one of the world's most successful technology companies, simply being the best and brightest isn't, by itself, enough to make one an effective leader. Overall, these eight traits reflect an effective leader who is courageous, builds relationships, and serves others. In addition, as noted by #7 (Have a clear vision and strategy for the team), a good leader must set the tone and cast the vision, which is also a part of establishing an effective culture.

While it's possible to identify the traits that effective leaders contribute to their cultures, it is also possible to identify characteristics and traits of ineffective leaders. In all honesty, the reason that people research and seek to identify what makes a good leader is because, unfortunately, the world has an ample supply of ineffective leaders. While you're certainly not reading this book to learn how to be a bad leader or department chair, you need to be aware of what contributes to an ineffective or toxic leader and/or employee. Being able to identify these traits will help you protect your department's culture and, most importantly, your people.

DARK TRIAD OF TOXIC BEHAVIORS

When asked about a company's toxic culture, Deborah Ancona, founder of the MIT Leadership Center, said it's difficult to spot both toxic leaders and employees because they are oftentimes popular and confident:

> Toxic leaders are often talking about all the great things they can do. People are attracted to that and see that as the kind of leader they want. Only later, through

interaction [with that person] or their behavior over time do you start to see the underbelly that isn't always visible at first glance.[10]

Ancona further states that toxic leaders or employees tend to exhibit a common set of traits referred to as the "dark triad" of personality disorders:[11]

1. Narcissism
2. Machiavellianism
3. Psychopathy

People with these traits can literally destroy an organization's culture and be detrimental to the professional and personal well-being of others. In addition, people who display these traits tend to be the office bullies as they are self-centered and lack empathy.[12] The following will provide a brief overview of each of the "dark triad" characteristics to better equip you as a leader to identify and address them appropriately.

Narcissism

Narcissistic individuals, despite being very charming and socially adept, lack empathy, manipulate others, and have no respect for rules or consequences. According to the *Diagnostic and Statistical Manual of Mental Disorders* (DSM-5), a source used by mental health professionals to diagnose mental health conditions, a person with narcissistic personality disorder has a grandiose sense of importance, oftentimes exaggerating, or lying about their achievements and social connections. They also have an unreasonable sense of entitlement and, as a result, will routinely take advantage of others to achieve their own goals. Above all, narcissistic individuals do not see anyone as their equal, frequently putting others down or needing to "one up" them.[13]

Narcissists can be hard to detect in the workplace since, on the surface, they appear to be charming and intelligent high-achievers. However, they can wreak havoc behind the scenes as they have little regard for rules, policies, and protocol and, above all, believe they are entitled, regardless of the cost or consequences.

Narcissists can be hard to detect in the workplace since, on the surface, they appear to be charming and intelligent high-achievers.

Machiavellianism

Machiavellianism is derived from the book *The Prince*, written by Italian author Niccolo Machiavelli in 1513, and describes a person who is sneaky, cunning, heartless, and driven by power and control. Similar to a narcissist, a Machiavellian can be very dishonest, deceitful and lack empathy for others. However, in addition to being able to control their emotions and present a calm and collected demeanor, another key trait of a Machiavellian is their ability to strategize, often long-term, in order to ultimately get what they want.

According to Dr. Mariana Bockarova, a researcher at the University of Toronto, Machiavellians can be the "greatest bullies of all" saying,

> The Machiavellian, who has perhaps had a healthy working relationship thus far with his or her colleague, which is possible for a Machiavellian until they see them to be of no use and may turn on them with no remorse, stealing every idea their colleague has had, spreading harsh rumors about their colleague hence cheating their way to the top, or even causing their colleague harm to gain that promotion, which fulfills all motivational attributes that are usually attractive to someone high in Machiavellianism.[14]

Leaders and employees who display traits of Machiavellianism can also be hard to detect since they can be charming, intelligent, and polite. In fact, they tend to be masters of flattery, and can appear as your best friend. Within an organizational setting, these people can also be very cliquish, using their deceitful prowess to establish an "in" and "out" group mentality, frequently pitting people against each other. This often involves the withholding of information to further control others and ultimately achieve their short and long-term goals.

Psychopathy

Similar to narcissists and Machiavellians, psychopaths can appear very normal, can be intelligent, well-liked, and able to charm your socks off. Although most people associate this term with criminals, according to Lilienfeld and Watts, "Most psychopaths aren't coldblooded or psychotic killers. Many of them live successfully among the rest of us, using their personality traits to get what they want in life, often at the expense of others."[15]

However, despite their charm and possible success, psychopaths tend to lack empathy, disregard rules and consequences, and can be highly manipulative. While they are usually able to present a calm demeanor, psychopaths find it difficult to deal with negative emotions and, consequently, are prone to severe outbursts of anger, which can include yelling at others.

Overall, the purpose of this brief overview of the dark triad of personality traits isn't to be negative and demeaning or to suggest that most people in higher education are toxic because they are not. On the contrary, it's precisely because of the fact that most people in most organizations are good, hard-working individuals that it's important to be aware of the small percentage who are truly toxic; they prey on and take advantage of the good people. Nonetheless, toxic individuals are poisonous to an organization, using charm and deception to silently erode its culture, like termites eating away at the foundation of a house.

As a department chair, you may not immediately know if there are toxic people in your department, even if you were an internal hire. It's possible that those who appeared to be your best friend and showered you with flattery and kindness as a professor may quickly turn on you once you become their chair. In fact, one informal indicator of a potentially toxic person is to see how they respond the first time you have to have a difficult conversation or tell them "no." While it's understandable if they're frustrated and unhappy, are they still professional or do they "blow up" either in front of you or behind the scenes?

To effectively work with someone who displays toxic traits, keep your distance and establish clearly defined boundaries.[16] As their leader, document every interaction you have with them and realize you may have to eventually bring it to the attention of your Dean and/or Human Resources Office.

Finally, as you work to develop relationships with others, thus gaining a sense of their true character, consider the following questions, which may also suggest someone who might possess one or more of the aforementioned toxic tendencies:

- Do they always follow protocol or have a knack for sidestepping the rules for which they claim ignorance or can provide what they consider a sound rationale?
- How do they respond to being told "no"?
- How do they respond to other forms of rejection, such as not being perceived as the best and brightest?
- Do they display a "look at me" mentality, bragging about accomplishments that are oftentimes embellished or made up?
- Can they genuinely compliment others without having to "one-up" them or say something to diminish their joy?
- How do they behave, one-on-one, with those they dislike, which are usually those who can see them as they really are? For example, do they make direct, and bold, threats that they later deny publicly and/or to their superiors? Do they simply avoid those who are honest and have integrity?

   The culture in which people work both affects and reflects their actions, beliefs, and values on a daily basis, all of which can be attributed to the leader. As the chair, you are the curator of your department's culture and your effectiveness as a leader will establish the type of culture in which your faculty and staff spend their professional lives. Although you can't control the types of people or personalities in your department, being aware of potential toxic traits can enable you to better serve everyone, thus enabling you to create a positive culture in which everyone feels safe and valued. Finally, an overall awareness of what makes up an effective culture will assist you in determining the culture you inherited along with the culture you wish to create. The following chapter will discuss how to assess the culture you inherit as a department chair.

Chapter 6

The Culture You Inherit

The first responsibility of a leader is to define reality.
—Max De Pree

Whether you are new to the university or have already been on campus as a professor, when you assume your role as department chair, you acquire a new perspective of your department's culture, like going from sitting atop a three-foot stool to looking out an airplane window at 30,000 feet. While you are not responsible for the culture you inherit, you are responsible for the culture you create, which is the lifeblood of any organization and must always be nurtured.

In fact, organizations without a defined and healthy culture are like numbers or statistics. By themselves, they're morally and emotionally neutral. However, once leaders add value, meaning, and context, they take on a life of their own and tell a story. The same can be said of your academic department. By itself, it's a flow chart, a list of names, phone numbers, emails, and offices. However, as the leader, you and your colleagues add value, meaning, and context. You affect, infuse, and maintain the culture. Ultimately, your organization will take on the values, norms, and behaviors that you promote on a daily basis.

Therefore, what makes up a healthy university department culture? How will you be able to learn more about the culture you inherit as a chair? To begin, it is possible to categorize organizational culture. In his book *Culture Renovation: 18 Leadership Actions to Build an Unshakeable Company*, Kevin Oakes provides the ten most common types of effective organizational cultures which tend to include the following leaders and employees:[1]

1. **Customer-Focused Culture**. Trustworthy and consultative leader with relationship-driven and productive employees

2. **Performance Culture**. Relentless, goal-oriented leader with merit-based competitive employees
3. **Innovative Culture**. Entrepreneurial and resourceful leader with creative and persistent employees
4. **Inclusive Culture**. Sincere and cooperative leader with diverse and relationship-focused employees
5. **Collaborative Culture**. Transparent and facilitator-style leader with open-minded and team-oriented employees
6. **Agile Culture**. Boundaryless and visionary leader with flexible and multitalented employees
7. **Purpose/Mission Culture**. Altruistic and philanthropical leader with compassionate and unselfish employees
8. **Learning Culture**. Intellectually curious and open-minded leader with aspirational and ambitious employees
9. **Quality Culture**. Systems-oriented and objective leader with compliant, risk-averse employees
10. **Safety Culture.** Procedural-oriented leader with compliant, risk-averse employees

Oakes also emphasizes the importance of leaders developing and maintaining culture, likening it to the renovation of a house, saying, "The unique traits need to be retained and the history should be honored."[2] Remember, as a leader, your first job is to define reality which means asking some critical questions that will help you to begin thinking about aspects of the culture that may need renovated.

For example, what is the department's foundation built upon? What it the history of the department, its place within the college, university, and community? What are the "badges of honor" people wear and the stories they continue to tell with pride? Who are some of the legends that have served as professors, administrators, and staff members? Overall, learn about the culture and history so you will have a better understanding of what people value and want to retain, modify, or possibly discard. The following sections offer some initial, getting-started advice that will help you better understand and appreciate the departmental culture you inherit as the chair.

GIVE CREDIT AND MOVE ON

As a chair, you could inherit a culture and follow a chair that falls anywhere on the spectrum between awesome and awful. Regardless of the situation you have come into, always give credit and acknowledge the work of your predecessor, thanking them for their contributions and then move on. It can be tempting to blame and complain but you're living in the present and were hired to take the department into the future. In addition, keep in mind that if you remain in higher education administration long enough, someone will eventually follow you so be kind and treat others as you would like to be treated.

LISTEN AND LEARN

The chair position provides a unique perspective. You will be able to see the fissures or cracks in the culture begin to surface and while you may initially have a good idea of what needs to be addressed, you must start by listening and learning. In addition to being visible and listening to others in informal settings, also make it a priority to schedule a meeting with each of your direct reports within the first two weeks of the semester. During these meetings, make it clear you just want to get to know them and the department better. Inform them that they are also free to share concerns as long as it's professional and doesn't unfairly represent another person. In other words, use these meetings to reinforce expectations for civil, professional behavior.

During these meetings, let your colleagues know that you will be taking some notes, not to be rude or to appear as though you are documenting everything but because what they say matters and it will enable you to follow up with them in the future. Finally, lead with courage and ask them what you need to hear, which could include some of the following:

- What are you passionate about?
- Why do you enjoy working here?
- How would you define the culture in this department?
- What is the foundation upon which this department was built?
- What do people in this department take pride in and want to carry forward?
- What are some things that might need to be renovated or discarded?
- Without disclosing identifiable details, tell me about your best and worst chairs or bosses and what made them that way?
- Keeping in mind that I'm only human and can't work miracles, what is it that you need me to do and be as your leader?
- What's the one thing that could change everything for you and this department? For example, if you were to come to campus tomorrow and your main source of professional frustration or stress were eliminated, what would that look like? What would have to realistically happen? (Note: realistically means it can neither be a miracle nor violate university policies or break any local, state, or federal laws.)

Taking the time to meet with your faculty and staff is an effective way for you to get to know them personally and also helps to better understand the history and current culture of the department along with the elements that should be retained, renovated, or possibly discarded.

KNOW YOUR ROSTER

To use an athletic coaching analogy, your roster, or the people you lead and serve (i.e., faculty and staff) are the only ones you're going to get for the foreseeable future, or at least the current academic year. Like a coach, these are the only athletes you have so if you're going to be successful, it must be with them. Besides, we are all human and there is no such thing as a perfect group of people so avoid a "wait and see and maybe there will be" mentality.

As a chair, you will never have a perfect group of people and they will never have a perfect leader. Like a coach, your job is to identify people's strengths and interests in order to provide the proper support, accountability, and resources so they can be successful.

> As a chair, you will never have a perfect group of people and they will never have a perfect leader.

Knowing your roster also means getting to know people in terms of their strengths, weaknesses, and goals. In almost every team sport, a good coach will know who can best serve the team in each position, as well as who is the next best person off of the bench. Everyone can contribute in some way and it's your job as the chair to know where people can be the most effective and fulfilled. For example, some of your faculty members will be more interested and talented in publishing articles or applying for grants while others may be more effective teachers. This also applies to how you may appoint or recommend people to committees or allocate funding for special training or conferences.

KEEP ASKING QUESTIONS

As you continue to assess the current status of your department's culture while getting to know people, keep asking great questions. In addition to the suggested questions you can ask face-to-face, another strategy is to send out a survey in which people can respond anonymously to questions that can provide additional insight into the culture. The following are suggestions for survey-style, open-ended questions and can provide insight into the culture you have inherited:

- I feel proud to be a part of the department when . . .
- I feel proud to be a part of this university when . . .
- My job is most enjoyable when . . .
- My job is most difficult when . . .
- I feel valued when . . .
- I don't feel valued when . . .
- I would describe our culture as . . .
- The part of our history that I am most proud of is . . .
- Moving forward, I think we should continue to do . . .
- Moving forward, I think we should not continue to do ...
- If I were the department chair for one day and could change one thing, I would . . .

While all surveys have inherited bias in terms of knowing if people are being honest or just saying what they think others want to hear, there is still value in surveying your faculty and staff. For example, this format provides a safe and anonymous platform to share their opinions and also gives you, as the chair, an opportunity to look for patterns and trends in their responses. In addition, this gives you the option of sharing the data with the department and possibly your Dean as an initial assessment of how people feel about the department's culture at a specific point in time.

CULTURE-KEEPERS AND CULTURE-KILLERS

Most organizations are made up of good, honest, and hard-working people who want to feel as though they matter, they're appreciated and can contribute in a meaningful way. Granted, as previously discussed, there can be a few "bad apples" here and there (i.e., the dark triad) but please understand that what follows is not to suggest that "Culture-Keepers" are the good people you inherited as chair and "Culture-Killers" are the bad ones. These are just terms used to help better analyze and assess the state of your department's culture.

People are what gives life to every organization, defining its culture by how they act and what they value on a daily basis. In addition, being in the people business is messy and complicated because, despite the best of intentions, no one is perfect. As a result, you will inherit a department that will have natural culture-keepers and culture-killers. As a chair, it will be your job to identify these people so you can keep the keepers and convert or divert the killers.

Culture-keepers are the individuals who support the overall mission and purpose of the department. They are like the departmental curators and sentinels whose daily actions and expressed values essentially represent the predominant organizational culture, always working to protect and promote their values while standing as gatekeepers to ensure nothing undesirable gets in. If you stood at the door to your building each morning and asked people if they were excited to be there, the culture-keepers would most likely say "yes."

Culture-keepers are the individuals who support the overall mission and purpose of the department.

The culture-killers, on the other hand, are not as eager to show up to the office each day and may not support the overall mission and purpose of the department. These individuals are not necessarily low-performers in terms of their teaching, scholarship, and service. Overall, the culture-killers simply do not align with the prevailing philosophy of the department which is another way of saying they are not overly supportive of the department's leadership. In fact, it could be that these individuals care deeply about the department and the university but simply felt ostracized by the previous leader, which could have been justified or the result of a misunderstanding.

Depending on the quality of the leader you are following, the keepers of the culture you inherit could be the killers of the culture you create and vice versa. To make things more complicated, the culture-keepers may desperately hope you maintain their way of life while the culture-killers will be praying for complete reformation. Either way, both parties are always very nice and eager to visit with you as soon as you are named the chair, thus contributing to a "honeymoon phase." In all honesty, you will meet some very kind and helpful people as you begin the chair position so take time to get to know them and build a relationship. In fact, as you get to know people, consider the following questions:

Who "Shows Up" Every Day?

In an academic department, this could be both literally and figuratively. For example, which people are always reliable, oftentimes on campus, in their office, especially on days when they have no on-campus commitments? In addition, what are they doing? This isn't to suggest you must be a micromanager and follow them around but honestly, what do they show up to do? These are also the people most likely to emerge when needed, especially if it's to serve others or in times of crisis.

Who Are the Influencers?

Similar to knowing who shows up every day, it's important to identify the natural influencers or leaders in the department. While they may also be those who "show up," it's not always the case so try to identify those who have or have had influence within the department, college, and/or university. For example, who are the gatekeepers of the promotion and tenure standards? Who are the "go-to" people for matters related to curriculum and assessment? When a job opens in the department or college, who is most likely to either serve on the committee or chair the search?

Who Has Been Unreasonably Empowered?

This applies to both faculty and staff. In every academic department there are those who, even with the best of intentions, have been unreasonably empowered beyond their job description. Sometimes this is because they have been there a long time and/or the previous chair directly empowered them.

For any organization to be successful, there are times when people have to go "above and beyond." However, there's a big difference between an administrative assistant who gives 110 percent each day, managing the office, answering the phone, and responding to emails and one who, with the best of intentions, tries to perform tasks that are not part of the job and should be handled by someone else.

As the chair, it is very important to not only identify the individuals who exceedingly go above and beyond, but to learn their actual job descriptions, which can be provided by the Human Resources Office. Once you have this information, schedule a meeting and let them know you appreciate the extra effort and while it shows great commitment to the department, you care too much to continue to ask them to unreasonably work beyond their job description.

How Deep Is the Authority?

How deep into the department do you have to ask questions or "dig" until you no longer find people reasonably empowered to make decisions and provide answers? While this may include those empowered beyond their job descriptions it is also an indicator of how tightly managed the previous culture was. Another way to look at this is to determine the highest level of decision people would be comfortable making without administrative approval. Although chairs are responsible for everything that happens in the department and there are some decisions that can only happen at the chair level or above, people should not be fearful of the consequences of answering questions that relate to their job description.

How Do People Respond to Being Told "No"?

This is rather simple to determine but can also be very insightful. While it's understandable that most people want to get their way and be told "yes" more than "no," it is also a reasonable expectation that people will accept the news and consequences as professionals. However, as evidenced by the dark triad of personality traits, people who become unreasonably upset and/or quietly vindictive (which is actually worse) when they don't get their way could potentially pose a problem to the overall culture of the department.

While there are many reasons for those who become unreasonably upset when they don't get their way, realize that this could be an indicator of the previous culture in which they were empowered and typically got what they wanted. It could also mean that, despite the previous, current, and future culture of the department, this is simply who they are. Either way, be mindful of whether or not there's a pattern of behavior among those who are told "no" as this could be a sign of future conflict. Nonetheless, continue to be supportive, always treating them professionally and with respect. However, establish boundaries and document encounters in which they become unreasonably upset in response to being told "no."

Who Are the Workaholics?

Also identify the individuals most likely to do everything, working themselves into the ground, simply so things will get done. This is certainly admirable and, at times, beneficial but it's not healthy. Usually, these people have great intentions and may believe that nothing will get done unless they do it. However, as a chair, it's your job to protect them from themselves while also creating a culture that doesn't naturally assume a few people will do all of the work.

BECAUSE OF OR IN SPITE OF?

Finally, in addition to the previous questions which can help you better understand the culture you inherit as a chair, you will also need to assess the overall productivity and related outcomes within the department, which will further reveal the status of your inherited culture. Asking if certain things occurred "because of" or "in spite of" the previous culture and leadership is very useful across a number of scenarios.

People are resilient creatures and while they perform better with effective leadership, don't assume that just because things seem fine that everything is running smoothly. Instead, ask if the outcome was because of or in spite of a positive and healthy culture, as supported by an effective leader.

For example, assume that at your university, over the course of twenty years (which represents three college presidents, four provosts, four deans within your college, and six department chairs) some of the major metrics, such as students' GPA, graduation rates, and scholarly productivity have all been consistently positive. Since it's a known fact that there were some not-so-good leaders at various levels within that twenty-year span, why worry about being a great chair because the data suggest things should be fine? This may be true, but have the students and faculty within the university, your college, and department been successful because of or in spite of the culture and leadership over the past two decades?

If previous success was because of the leadership, then you can be confident that people were working in an environment that enabled them to strive for their maximum potential. However, accomplishments and success that are primarily in spite of the culture and leadership, while still noteworthy, should also cause disappointment and regret because, unfortunately, faculty, staff, and students were not working in an environment conducive to reaching their maximum potential.

Leadership matters. Culture matters. Step back and look at both the accomplishments, strengths, and weaknesses of your department and ask if it was because of or in spite of the culture you have inherited. Were people successful because they felt comfortable and valued or was everything uphill and required working around certain people, policies, and politics?

Although you cannot control the departmental culture you inherit as a chair, you can still work as an archeologist, uncovering clues and artifacts, primarily through listening, observing, and asking great questions, which will enable you to better understand and appreciate the culture you inherit.

Chapter 7

The Culture You Create

Culture eats strategy for breakfast
—Peter Drucker

Recall from chapter 4 that once you become a leader your daily agenda isn't completely your own and, more importantly, it's not all about you. As the chair, part of being the 24/7 walking advertisement for your department means you are the main cheerleader; if you don't have anything to cheer about, neither will anyone else. You are always the chair, on and off campus. Each and every day, everything you do and say represents you, your department, and all its stakeholders. Because of this, your daily actions, based upon what you value, will ultimately contribute to the culture you create.

GETTING STARTED

Chapter 1 presented a process designed to identify your purpose and reasons for leading, which hopefully is at the intersection of your passion, talents, and profession. Take some time to review these reasons and your mission statement. Say them out loud, write them down, and place them on the wall or wherever they will be front and center and force you to focus on their value. In addition, answer the following questions:

- What are the inherent values and behaviors that you must live out each day to reflect your mission and purpose?
- Based on your mission and purpose, how will you address conflict and difficult decisions?

- Given enough time, if those in your department were shown your mission and purpose and asked if it aligns with your character, what would they say?
- What does your mission and purpose say about the type of culture you will create and promote as a leader?
- What type of people will be attracted to this mission and purpose?
- If lived out each day, what will your mission and purpose enable others to do and/or become?
- If you could stand in front of your building each morning and ask people in your department to describe the culture in which they work, what would you want them to say?
- Is there alignment between your mission and purpose and your "non-negotiables" or that which you would be willing to resign over or be fired for?

In addition, even though the culture you create is a collaborative process, it is still helpful to establish some basic expectations from the beginning, which should also be reiterated during your first official department meeting. This is not a form of poor leadership or micromanagement but rather shares expectations that are in line with who you are and what you believe as a leader.

For example, a few common expectations within an academic department could be to always do what's best for students, treat each other with kindness, honesty, and professionalism, realizing that everyone is human and makes mistakes. Here are a few other suggestions to share about yourself with your department, thus relaying your leadership philosophy and signaling the type of culture you will create:

- What is your leadership philosophy?
- How do you view and approach conflict?
- How will you communicate with the department?
- How do you define character?
- How do you approach and make difficult decisions?
- How do you prefer to build relationships and get to know others?

Although it can take some time to understand the culture you inherited, as a chair, you started building your own culture from the moment you accepted the job. Every interaction and encounter matters.

What Did You Hear and Learn?

Chapter 6 focused on ways to identify and better understand the department culture you inherited, which is still important, even if you were an internal hire. Nonetheless, what did you learn from listening to others, both formally and informally? What type of picture does it paint of the current culture and how does it coincide with your mission and who you are as a leader? For example, do people enjoy being in the department and feel valued and appreciated? What were some of the common words people used to talk about what they enjoyed and what they would change? What was the one thing that could change everything?

In addition, if you chose to send out a survey, what were the results? What makes people proud to be a part of the department and the university? Are there specific aspects of the department's history that should be retained? Are there parts of the history or common practices that people feel should be changed? Finally, if people could serve as the chair for one day, what would they do?

All organizations have flaws and room for improvement; academic departments in higher education are no exception. Do not discredit your perceptions of the positive and negative aspects of the culture as they tend to be valid, especially within your first ninety days. Step back and take into consideration all that you have learned and continue to learn as it will help to identify potential fissures in the organization which may need addressed. Also realize that by virtue of being the chair, you inherently represent a change and people can oftentimes be fearful of change. The following, attributed to King Whitney Jr., eloquently frames how people view change:

> Change has a considerable psychological impact on the human mind. To the fearful it is threatening because it means that things may get worse. To the hopeful it is encouraging because things may get better. To the confident it is inspiring because the challenge exists to make things better.[1]

What vision of the future will you provide for your department and how will you convey that it's safe and provides an opportunity for improvement?

The Renovation

In his book *Culture Renovation: 18 Leadership Actions to Build an Unshakeable Company*,[2] Kevin Oakes likens the cultural change within an organization to renovating an old house. For example, the first step is to make sure the house was built on a firm foundation and has a sound infrastructure or "good bones." In addition, it's important to learn about the history of the house along with its location. What are the unmistakable, non-negotiable characteristics that must be maintained, even if it requires a great deal of repair? Furthermore, what needs to be updated? For example, homes built in the early 1900s, if still standing today, eventually had to be wired for Internet capabilities. Finally, what aspects of the house need to be discarded, primarily because they are beyond repair or are not essential to its core characteristics?

As a chair, please know that you will not be faced with nor should you truly renovate (i.e., destroy and rebuild) anything. Hardworking people spent a significant amount of time, with the best of intentions, creating something of which they are very proud. However, the concept of a renovation can still be helpful since it can provide illuminating, guiding questions moving forward. Therefore, pose the following questions to people within your department, which can be done through a combination of informal and formal settings, both one-on-one and in groups:

- What is the foundation of our department? What makes us unique?
- What is the history and legacy of our department? What are some of our successes over the years? What are we known for?
- If we had to pick a few areas in need of refurbishing or a tune-up, what would they be?
- What needs to be done or accomplished for the first time? What needs to be permanently changed?
- 3-2-1 Question: List three things we should hold on to, two things to refurbish, and one thing we might want to reconsider or reevaluate.

While there are many scenarios within higher education, it's possible that an academic department, when asked these questions, might say that their foundation is that they were one of the original departments when the university was founded over 100 years ago. This is obviously a defining characteristic and something to be proud of and worthy of preservation. Likewise, when asked what needs to be reconsidered, it could be that, for years, the department has held on to practices for reaching out to potential students that, over time, have become outdated and no longer resonate with eighteen-year-old adolescents. These are rather simple examples but, overall, it is important to go through the renovation process.

CULTURE CONSIDERATIONS

In addition to the formal and informal conversations and messages you send to those in your department, especially as it relates to who you are as a leader and the shared culture you hope to create, the following topics are additional considerations that you may want to first internalize for yourself and then share with your faculty and staff.

Honesty and Transparency

While it is always necessary for leaders to be honest and transparent, this question and requirement is especially embedded within higher education. This will undoubtedly be asked a few times during the interview process but, in addition, it's important to share with your department how you define and embody these terms.

Transparency isn't telling everyone everything every minute of every day. This may be a bit of an exaggeration but there are those in every organization that feel they must know everything about everyone and the extent to which they haven't been told (or in their minds, lied to) is a measure of how honest and transparent their leader is. If, as a department chair, you were to share everything with everyone, ranging from personnel issues to student information, you would be violating protocol and not displaying sound character and integrity.

> Transparency isn't telling everyone everything every minute of every day.

So how is it possible to be an honest and transparent leader when, despite what some may expect, you can't truly be an open book and share everything? Does this mean you have to be dishonest and lie? Absolutely not. When discussing how to be an honest and transparent leader, leadership author Craig Groeschel says, "Telling the truth means that what you say is true. It doesn't mean that everything true needs to said."[3] In other words, share with your faculty that while you will always tell them the truth, thus being honest and transparent, there will be some things that, while true, you simply cannot share. This doesn't mean you're dishonest and lack transparency, it means you have integrity and can be trusted, especially with confidential information.

Honest and transparent leaders are also consistent. If true character is who you are when you think no one else is watching, then being honest and transparent means being consistent and predictable when no one else is watching. This may upset people at times. However, even when people are upset or disappointed with their leader, they should still not be surprised by the behavior, knowing that their actions and decisions are consistent and in line with their character, which is positive, honest, and supportive.

Motivation

Although the topic of motivation has been addressed in previous chapters, it is worth mentioning within the context of the culture you will create as a department chair. In his bestselling book *Drive: The Surprising Truth About What Motivates Us*, Daniel Pink challenges the old "carrot and stick" notion of extrinsic motivation suggesting that people are more intrinsically motivated by the following three elements: [4]

1. Autonomy—the desire to direct our own lives
2. Mastery—the urge to make progress and get better at something that matters
3. Purpose—the yearning to do what we do in the service of something larger than ourselves

As a department chair, you may have a slight advantage over leaders outside of higher education because the tenure-track offers people an ample amount of autonomy. In addition, those who have terminal degrees have certainly mastered their academic field, thus enabling them to pursue their purpose. Nonetheless, it is important to be aware of these three elements and the extent to which you can create a culture that communicates and supports their respective values.

Autonomy

People should feel as though they have some control or ownership of their work which also suggests they have ownership of the organizational culture. Within your department, this could mean you send the message that you trust people to do their jobs so you will not micromanage or treat them poorly but instead, be supportive while also holding them accountable. For example, if the university has asked all departments to update their curriculum and assessments for accreditation purposes, you can appoint people to this committee. Additionally, you can make it clear that while there are timelines and expectations, you trust they can do the job and you will support them however you can.

Mastery

In addition to having a reasonable amount of autonomy, people should also feel like they have the skills and potential to be successful, which includes the belief they can always learn and improve. Even though many of the people within your department will have mastered their field through advanced degrees and related accomplishments, life in higher education requires the acquisition of new skills and the ability to adapt. Therefore, send the message that you know they are capable and will continue to grow and be successful in the future. Overall, let them know you believe in their abilities to provide a great effort, which includes giving them permission to fail.

Purpose

Most people in your department will understand their general purpose (i.e., job description and expectations) but must also understand that what they do is more than just a job and contributes to something bigger than themselves. This starts by adopting and communicating an "anti-justa" clause. Quite simply, those whom you serve are never "justa" professor, secretary, advisor, and so on. On the contrary, they are much more than their job title, they are an integral part of your department and its greater purpose which is primarily to serve students. No matter the academic content of your department, it takes a village to be successful and, as a result, everyone in your department matters and has a purpose.

Courage and Conflict

Courage and conflict go hand in hand and are woven into the fabric of leadership. As a leader establishing your vision and culture, it's important to send the message that you are courageous and will not shy away from conflict. This is not to suggest that you have to be overpowering and intimidating to get this point across. Simply let people know through your words and actions that you are there to serve them which means leading with courage and addressing conflict.

A significant part of establishing and communicating a culture of courage, as defined by actions and values, is to realize that you encourage what you tolerate and normalize what you ignore. As the department chair, everything you do, or don't do, sends a message and has a consequence that over time will determine your true culture.

You encourage what you tolerate and normalize what you ignore.

While it may be temporarily more comfortable to tolerate or put up with a faculty member who always tries to dominate meetings, in doing so you are sending a direct message to everyone, including those who are annoyed by the behavior, that it will be tolerated while encouraging the faculty member to keep doing it. Given enough time, tolerating or ignoring the behavior makes it a normal and accepted (albeit annoying and uncomfortable) part of your culture. Bestselling author and consultant John Amaechi sums it up with the following: "Culture is defined by the worst behavior tolerated."[5]

Related to encouraging what's tolerated and normalizing what's ignored is the ability to understand and differentiate between a cause and a symptom.

As a chair, you will sometimes feel like "Dr. Fix-It" because everyone wants you to help solve or fix problems. While it may not be natural to want to lean into problems, it's your job, choosing courage over comfort. You can deal with the problem or the problem will deal with you. Either way, it's not going away. Therefore, always try to identify if the problem at hand is a cause or a symptom.

Usually, problems are a symptom of another problem and not the stand-alone cause. As a leader, you get one opportunity to treat the true cause. After that, it grows and becomes a symptom of a problem you caused by tolerating and ignoring it. Leaders who continually ignore problems eventually become the problem.

For example, as a first-year chair, a faculty member comes to you and says they feel as though they were not treated fairly as part of their third-year promotion and tenure review, which occurred before you started. It's safe to say you didn't cause this problem but, from a larger perspective, what did cause this? Was the third-year review written correctly, meaning the true cause is that the person is simply upset it didn't go their way or were they, for some reason, targeted and unfairly treated, thus suggesting it's a symptom of a deeper problem?

Unfortunately, the problems you deal with will not all be as simple as the previous example. However, despite the perceived severity or simplicity, still work to determine if the problems you are asked to fix are a cause or a symptom. It takes courage but your decision to address problems appropriately will contribute to the quality and sustainability of your department's culture.

A final note on courage is that it's a permanent characteristic, you either have it every day or you don't have it all. Leaders who are only courageous in desperate times are just acting out of desperation. For example, it takes courage to tell someone their behavior is unprofessional and unacceptable. It takes courage to adopt a policy that, while it's best for the students, may temporarily upset a few faculty or staff members. However, waiting to stand up and do something only when times are desperate, such as finally deciding to adopt an initiative because enrollment suddenly dropped and the budget has been cut, isn't courage, it's veiled desperation.

As a leader, it's also admirable to show vulnerability and apologize and admit when you're wrong because (1) it's the right thing to do and (2) your people will know you're wrong whether you admit it or not. However, in addition to apologizing and admitting you were wrong, take steps to make it right. For example, as a first-year chair, Dr. Newchair made the quick decision to do away with a student-based organization that was very popular. Now, three years later, Dr. Newchair realizes he never should have done this. It's admirable for him to admit his mistake but he should also take steps to fix it, such as reinstating the group.

Shared Experiences

As part of being in a department with a developing, shared culture, you are also a family, spending a good portion of your waking hours in the same place. Before people can take ownership of the departmental culture, they must first develop relationships. These connections can still be professional and don't have to cross any personal boundaries but, in the end, they are necessary. One way to do this is through shared experiences.

Shared experiences can take on a number of forms that naturally occur within a department such as meetings, luncheons, or informal conversations around the water cooler or coffee pot. In addition, people within your department may also choose to interact together outside of the office. As a leader, it's a delicate balance because, like any relationship, these experiences cannot be forced and you certainly can neither tell nor require people to interact socially outside of the office. However, pay attention to how people informally interact within the department. For example, consider the following:

- What's the tone or feel of the room before a meeting officially starts? Are people voluntarily talking to each other? Is there laughter?
- When faculty are in their offices, are their doors open? How often are people just dropping by offices, having conversations in the doorway?
- When faculty go to other offices, are they using a hushed or secretive tone? How often does it result in a closed-door meeting?
- Are people generally cordial and greet each other in public spaces?

In addition to observing how people interact, thus revealing the quality of their shared experiences, model positive behavior as a chair. For example, is the main department office always open and inviting? Even though you may, at times, need to close your personal office door, if you happen to have a larger space to welcome people, such as in an office suite, it's important that this be open, positive, and welcoming.

While it might seem like a chore to be interrupted by a faculty member in the office as you go out to ask the administrative assistant a question, remember that you are always modeling and promoting your vision and culture. Therefore, take time to visit with people. Let others hear an acceptable amount of noise or laughter coming from the main office. Do not underestimate the importance of the messages, both directly and indirectly, that are sent from the physical space or spaces that constitute the department.

Finally, while it's somewhat common for organizations, including university departments, to have retreats where everyone gets together in the same space for an entire day to accomplish a task (such as developing curriculum or a mission statement), do these for the right reasons with stated objectives so that everyone will know their time is valued.

Overall, shared experiences are a necessary ingredient to building and sustaining a positive organizational culture. While you cannot force people into authentic, shared experiences, you can provide opportunities for faculty and staff to communicate and collaborate in formal and informal settings.

Difficult Conversations

Even after you have a better understanding and appreciation of the culture you have inherited and, subsequently, hope to create, there will still be some who seem unwilling to contribute and may be difficult. One way to look at this is to ask yourself the following: How many difficult, yet constructive, conversations stand between you and the culture you hope to create? Not only does this remove the person from the problem but it also clearly identifies what must be done in the service of others.

> How many difficult conversations stand between you and the culture you hope to create?

In the end, the culture of your department is a direct reflection of the collective values and behaviors you and your colleagues promote and display on a daily basis. Although you will have a general idea of the culture and vision of your department, you must also take the time to ask questions, get to know people, and let them know you. Be willing to learn and understand the history of the department and the university, viewing any change in culture as a renovation in which you preserve the past and possibly refurbish other essential components. Culture matters and represents where people live and work, which contributes to their happiness and enables them to reach their maximum potential.

Chapter 8

Conflict Preparation

*Give me six hours to chop down a tree and I will spend the first four
sharpening the axe.*

—Abraham Lincoln

As the leader of your department, you will have to address some type of
conflict every day. If ignored, conflicts never go away but continue to grow
day-by-day. Furthermore, if approached correctly, conflict can be a necessary, constructive component to your department's stability, growth, and
success. As Margaret Heffernan said, "For good ideas and true innovation,
you need human interaction, conflict, argument, debate."[1]

If ignored, conflicts never go away but continue to grow day-by-day.

Although this all sounds reasonable, the harsh reality is that conflict is
uncomfortable, it's scary, and, for most people, it's not normal. Even so, as
the chair, dealing with conflict is as much a part of your job as scheduling
classes and replying to your dean's emails.

Conflict doesn't necessarily have to be synonymous with combat or fight-
ing. Granted, most associate conflict with these negative outcomes, doing
just about everything they can to avoid it. However, within the scope of
an organization's culture, constructive conflict is a necessary component, a
way of renegotiating the terms of the various relationships that exist among
individuals and groups. In fact, very few significant initiatives, programs, or

changes occur in a vacuum, void of conflict. Therefore, if you hope to serve your department as an effective leader and change agent, you're going to have to accept and embrace conflict.

CONFLICT AND DRAMA

Before moving on, it's important to define and establish an understanding of the words conflict and drama. These two words frequently work hand in hand and can be used synonymously, especially within academic departments in higher education.

Conflict is defined as "competitive or opposing action of incompatibles; antagonistic state or action (as of divergent ideas, interests, or persons)"[2] and a "mental struggle resulting from incompatible or opposing needs, drives, wishes, or external or internal demands."[3] In other words, conflict is not necessarily a battle and isn't inherently uncomfortable. Conflict is simply an opposition of viewpoints, ideas, and interests both internally and externally among individuals. Two or more people can be in conflict or a single person can be in conflict with themselves, most likely trying to reconcile something from their past or attempting to make a future decision.

Drama is defined as "a state, situation, or series of events involving interesting or intense conflict of forces."[4] Over time, this term has evolved, referring to conflict-causing behavior that is intentional and frequently with malice. For example, someone who constantly spreads false rumors and pits people against each other could be said to be creating or causing a lot of drama. In addition, an individual who is consistently negative, upset, and tells the whole world about it could also be causing drama and referred to as "dramatic."

Addressing conflict each day doesn't mean that it will always be high-stakes and high-stress but it will still require constant attention. Think of conflict and drama within your department as a fire that's always burning and can't be ignored. On one end of the spectrum, if managed properly, the fire is small and harmless, and simply smolders. With a bit of attention, there's a small chance it will ignite and become unmanageable. On the other end of the conflict-drama, spectrum is a raging fire that is likely out of control and requires professional firefighters. While there are always a few, spontaneous, unavoidable fires in the life of every leader, most start as small, smoldering fires that, if not ignored, could have been avoided.

The best way to minimize conflict and drama is to address small problems on a daily basis before they grow exponentially. A day without conflict of any kind should be worrisome. As anyone who has worked with children can attest, although it can be stressful when they are making a lot of noise running around playing, you should really be concerned when, all of a sudden, it becomes quiet. The same is true in leadership. While it may be a bit stressful or downright annoying when people are "making noise" every day, it's a sign of a normal, healthy, functioning department. However, if it becomes quiet and you have a day without any problems to solve, you should be worried.

THE LIFE CYCLE OF A PROBLEM

Even though you can't eradicate or avoid all conflict and drama, you can work to minimize and manage it. The best way to predict someone's future is to look at their daily activities because they are what they repeatedly do. Therefore, the most effective way to be proactive and either extinguish or keep the smoldering fire of conflict under control is to understand the life cycle of a problem.

Although some problems truly come out of nowhere, many problems can be minimized or avoided. Problems will come in many shapes and sizes and from all types of stakeholders. Some problems will be simple and others will have the potential to turn into real disasters. As mentioned in chapter 7, most problems are either an initial cause or a symptom of something else. The goal is to prevent or extinguish a smoldering fire by addressing the root cause of the problem so it won't grow into a larger fire that will be harder to contain.

Problems, which are the seeds of conflict and drama, are usually the result of poor decisions, poor communication, and/or unmet, unrealistic expectations. As soon as you are aware of the problem, it's like you are holding a seed in your hand. Since conflict is unavoidable as soon as a problem comes up, your best choice is to address the problem head-on, thus controlling and reducing the severity of conflict. However, if you choose your own comfort over courage and ignore the problem, which is akin to sewing that seed, it will only grow and become worse. What takes more effort? Telling someone you won't plant a tree or chopping one down?

The minute you choose to ignore (i.e., nurture) a problem, it will continue to produce more problems, which means more conflict and drama. Furthermore, as the person who sewed that seed by failing to address the initial problem, you are now part of the problem's life cycle. Ultimately, you have caused a new problem by ignoring the first problem, which will also continue to sprout other problems. Unnecessary and enhanced conflict and drama are the fruits of ignored problems.

For example, it is brought to your attention that one of your faculty members, Dr. Veneer, has been eloquently shirking their duties as the department's curriculum coordinator, making junior faculty do their work under the guise that they are mentoring them and providing a valuable experience for their promotion and tenure files. Make no mistake, when it's time to submit reports or receive any type of public acknowledgment, Dr. Veneer is more than happy to take the credit. However, Dr. Stalwart, the ranking member of your department, has found out, isn't happy about it and brings it to your attention.

As soon as you are made aware of the problem, you are holding the seed and have a choice to make, which will determine the level of conflict you must address. It's a simple decision. If you choose to address the problem head-on by visiting with Dr. Veneer and establishing expectations, you will minimize the problem, ensuring it will not grow into something bigger and more difficult to manage. However, if you ignore the problem, you have now (1) planted a seed that will sprout more conflict and drama and (2) created a new problem by ignoring the first problem. If ignored, problems never truly go away. Instead, they grow, expand, and mutate into something far greater than the original cause.

PREPARING TO ADDRESS CONFLICT

Even though you can take steps to minimize and manage conflict, it still must be addressed, which can be uncomfortable. Fortunately, it's possible to become comfortable with these uncomfortable conversations. However, it's important to realize that you will undoubtedly upset some people through addressing conflict and could even make a few enemies. You must accept this because you can't lead and keep everyone happy at the same time. Luckily, this isn't a new phenomenon.

Victor Hugo, French poet, novelist, and author of *Les Misérables*, published a diary in the mid-nineteenth century in which he recounts his meeting with Abel François Villemain, a French educator and politician. In a now-famous (and oftentimes misattributed) quote, Hugo says,

> You have enemies? Why, it is the story of every man who has done a great deed or created a new idea. It is the cloud which thunders around everything which shines. Fame must have enemies, as light must have gnats. Do not bother yourself about it; disdain. Keep your mind serene as you keep your life clear. Do not give your enemies the satisfaction of thinking that they cause you grief or pain. Be happy, be cheerful, be disdainful, be firm.[5]

While some of this may seem a bit harsh for the politics of twenty-first-century higher education, it still holds applicable wisdom. Hugo is saying that nothing of great consequence or of lasting value has or can ever be accomplished by keeping everyone happy. As a leader, it's not possible to make everyone happy with every decision; there will frequently be those who disagree with you personally and/or professionally. However, it's one of the many costs associated with leadership.

Pre-conflict Checklist

In aviation, all pilots, regardless of their experience or the size of the aircraft, must perform a prefight checklist before every takeoff to ensure that nothing goes wrong in the air that could have been prevented while on the ground. To address conflict and drama, you ultimately have to have a conversation with another person. No matter how experienced you are with conflict or the size of the problem you're addressing, always go through the following checklist of questions and reminders before you "take off" and communicate, thus minimizing the number of preventable mistakes.

- Seven, nine, crime, or dime?
- Why do you lead?
- Whom do you serve?
- Have you built relationships?
- Do your homework.
- Transpose the problem.
- Reflect your culture.
- Choose courage.
- Rationalize your fear.

Seven, Nine, Crime, or Dime?

Title VII of the Civil Rights Act of 1964 "prohibits employment practices that discriminate because of race, color, national origin, sex (including pregnancy, sexual orientation, and gender identity) and religion."[6] Title IX of the Education Amendments of 1972 was enacted to ensure that "no person in the United States shall, on the basis of sex, be excluded from participation in, be denied the benefits of, or be subjected to discrimination under any education program or activity receiving Federal financial assistance."[7]

As a higher education administrator, you must analyze and assess all problems and sources of potential conflict to determine the severity and whether or not you need to immediately report the issue to upper administration and/ or the proper authorities. This is not a legal phrase and certainly should not be taken as legal advice. However, asking if a problem or source of conflict involving students, faculty, and/or staff violates Title VII, Title IX, is any type of crime or involves the inappropriate or questionable use of money (i.e., dimes) can reveal situations that you should not address on your own and must immediately report. In fact, you can be found personally liable for withholding or failing to report certain information so when in doubt, err on the side of caution and follow your university's reporting protocol.

Fortunately, the majority of problems, conflict and drama that you address on a daily basis will neither involve crimes nor violate protected rights but instead, will represent common issues and misunderstandings that frequently occur in an academic department. Therefore, once you are certain you can address the issue on your own, continue with the following "pre-conflict" checklist.

Why Do You Lead?

Go back to your purpose, mission statement, and reasons for being a leader. Reflect upon these and remind yourself of the bigger picture and why you are in your current role. For example, if your mission or purpose is to lead with honesty and compassion, then make sure you embody those characteristics when you have the conflict conversation. If the roles were reversed, what type of chair would you want to have and how would you prefer to be treated?

Whom Do You Serve?

While you serve and lead the person with whom you will address the conflict, you also serve and lead everyone else, which means you are always "talking out of both side of your mouth.". This doesn't mean you are dishonest, it means that when you communicate or send a message to *one* person, it also sends a message to *every* person. Therefore, you are not only communicating with the person associated with the conflict but, at the same time, you're also sending a message to everyone else in the department. For example, if you tell a faculty member they don't have to come to work, those who take pride in being present each day may feel as though you don't appreciate them.

The last person you should be serving in a conflict is yourself on a personal level, which means any previous issues you've had with the person or personal opinions or agenda should not come into play. Also remember that people are your business, which means you must accept others and yourself as flawed, imperfect beings. The people business can be messy but, in the end, everyone deserves to be treated fairly and professionally, which frequently involves extending them grace and the benefit of the doubt.

Have You Built Relationships?

Although you can't play favorites and treat some better than others, ask yourself if you have put in the work to develop a positive, working relationship with the other person involved in the upcoming conversation. How much do you know about this person? What are their strengths and goals? What are some areas in which they could use some additional support or coaching? Are they naturally combative or do they simply agree with anything you tell them? Have they been involved with a similar type of conflict before and if so, can you find a positive aspect to help address the current issue?

The best way to avoid a misunderstanding with someone is to start with a positive relationship in which you understand and appreciate each other. Therefore, how well do you know this person and to what extent can that make a potentially uncomfortable conversation easier?

Do Your Homework

Regardless of their size and severity, all conflicts have associated documents such as emails or even what's written in someone's contract or the university's negotiated agreement. In addition, there are frequently the viewpoints and recollections of others that you need to be aware of. Therefore, before initiating the conversation, make sure you have all of the available facts and have reviewed any relevant policies so you know the parameters in which you can operate and can also answer potential questions. At times, this may involve consulting your Dean, Human Resources Office, or, with administrative approval, the university's general counsel.

To further prepare, take time to write out some of the essential questions you need to ask and subsequent understandings that must occur as a result of the conversation. If you still feel unprepared, ask a trusted friend or colleague to role-play the scenario with you, making sure not to disclose any confidential information.

Transpose the Problem

To ensure fairness and to confirm that you are being consistent with your expectations and subsequent consequences, transpose the problem to a different person. For example, how would you feel and behave if you were to address the same problem with the person in your department least likely to be in this situation? How would you behave during the conversation if you knew your Dean or Provost were either in the room or would later view a recording of the session? Transposing the problem and your responses to different people can help remove unintended bias to ensure fair and professional treatment.

Reflect Your Culture

Addressing conflict contributes to the type of culture you create and promote as a leader. In some ways, the culture of your department is shaped one conflict at a time. (Remember asking how many difficult conversations it would take to change the culture?) Therefore, reflect on the overall purpose of the conversation and make sure your words, actions, and treatment of the other person are in line with your character and the culture you want to create.

The culture of your department is shaped one conflict at a time.

Choose Courage

One of the reasons that some people in higher education claim to have no interest in administrative roles, saying "you couldn't pay me enough to do that," is primarily due to the thought of dealing with problems and addressing conflict through uncomfortable and awkward conversations. They're not entirely wrong. It's going to be uncomfortable and would be temporarily easier to avoid it altogether. However, the life cycle of a problem dictates you can either deal with the issue now, when it's still manageable, or wait until it's out of control. Therefore, do what's best for your department and those you serve by choosing courage over your personal comfort.

Rationalize Your Fear

Remember that leaders earn their money on the difficult days, choosing to walk into uncomfortable, fearful situations that others prefer to avoid. Anyone can have a pleasant, positive conversation with another person or decide between two, equally good options. However, it takes courage to show up on the bad days and have uncomfortable conversations and make decisions for which there are no good options, only varying levels of consequence, ridicule, and critique. Therefore, leading with courage means you must identify, acknowledge, and rationalize your fears, which ultimately means addressing the question of "What am I afraid of?"

If you have gone through the previous steps on the checklist, ensuring that the conflict you are about to address doesn't need to be reported or moved higher up the chain of command, you have worked to remove any unintentional bias, done your homework and collected all relevant materials, have some level of professional relationship with the person, and, above all, commit to treating them with honesty, compassion, and professionalism, you have very little to fear. This is still easier said than done as the thought of conflict is scary and can cause anxiety, ranging from how others will perceive you to potential implications on your job performance and security.

Yet, despite your best efforts and impeccable professionalism, a person or group of people could still disagree with you and try to make life difficult because you did your job and addressed a problem. However, what's the worst they can do? Gossip, rumors, and whisper campaigns are the tactics of those who lack a solid argument. When people can't find fault in your actions or how you have done your job, all they have left to attack and try to control is how other people see you. Perhaps former British prime minister Margaret Thatcher summed it up best saying, "I always cheer up immensely if an attack is particularly wounding because I think, well, if they attack one personally, it means they have not a single political argument left."[8]

The good news, however, is that most of your fears about the potential consequences of conflict are irrational. Besides, you cannot control what other people think and say about you and if you're their leader, you have to love them anyway. Therefore, continue to choose courage daily, embracing your fear and addressing conflict head-on, which will be discussed more in-depth in the next chapter.

Chapter 9

Addressing Conflict

Conflict is inevitable but combat is optional.
—Max Lucado

The previous chapter provided an overview of conflict, situated within an academic department. The life cycle of a problem illustrates how, if ignored, problems will continue to grow. Therefore, it's best to address problems and associated conflict early and often so that they don't transform into something more significant and harder to control.

In addition, conflict takes courage, with means you will most likely upset a few people and even make an enemy or two along the way. Nonetheless, it is possible to mitigate the severity and consequences of conflict by going through the pre-conflict checklist which helps to identify the proper protocol for addressing the issue along with ensuring you are well-prepared and mindful of any unintentional bias or unprofessional behavior.

Even with the best preventative measures, there will always come a point where the *rubber meets the road* and, as part of your job description, you must address the problem and related conflict through having a conversation. Make no mistake, it can be scary and cause anxiety but with additional preparation and considerations, you can be the leader your department needs and effectively, professionally, and efficiently lean into the conflict.

While there are a number of ways you will most likely engage in some difficult conversations, ranging from one-on-one with a faculty member to addressing a larger group, the following guiding principles are applicable across all contexts.

GET IT RIGHT VS. BEING RIGHT

According to Brené Brown, part of being a daring, courageous leader is shifting from a mindset of always wanting to "be right" and instead, working to "get it right."[1] This means entering the conversation with an open mind and a willingness to seek understanding and "get it right" by doing the right thing for everyone involved. This doesn't mean you cannot be firm and hold people accountable; it simply suggests you will respect the other person and, if necessary, admit your own faults and shortcomings. In the end, seek to better understand and acknowledge the other person's reality because that's the world they live in.

Getting it right also means making sure there are no ambiguities or misunderstandings. Accordingly, there are two common sets of words that should always be clarified, preferably quantified, when spoken within a conflict-related conversation: Everyone and No One; Always and Never.

Everyone and No One

Always ask for clarification when someone uses either of these words. For example, "Everyone says this is the right decision." Define everyone. Does that mean everyone on campus, everyone in the department, or everyone the person has talked to over the last twelve hours which can be quantified as two people? Likewise, someone might say, "No one thinks we should do this." Define no one. Does this mean not a single person in the world, on campus, in the department or they simply have yet to find someone who thinks this is a good idea?

Always and Never

Again, ask for clarification for both of these terms as it is unlikely accurate. For example, a student calls your office and says, "Dr. Z never returns my emails." Define never. To start, when was the last time they sent Dr. Z an email and how much time has passed since then? Overall, how many times this semester have they sent Dr. Z an email and, on average, how long do they take to reply?

Additionally, a faculty member comes to your office and says, "People always ignore my opinions." Alright, define always. Does this mean that since this person has been on campus their opinions have been ignored each and every time? Over the past year, month, or even week, how many times have they had their opinions shot down, by whom, and what was the context and/or supporting rationale?

ADDRESS THE PROBLEM, NOT THE PERSON

This may seem rather logical but when anxiety and tensions are high, it can be natural to slip into a competitive, self-preservation mode and directly attack the person instead of the problem. Recall from a previous chapter that you must lead with love, even if you are not necessarily fond of the other person. Therefore, communicate that anything you discuss, along with subsequent expectations and/or consequences will be in response to the person's behavior and a willingness to help them improve and in no way suggests they are a bad human being. Good people can make poor choices. Always separate the behavior from the individual.

BE DIRECT WITH YOUR INTENTIONS AND WORDS

Regardless of the topic or circumstances, let the other person know up-front that even though this may be an uncomfortable conversation, your goal is to respect them, both personally and professionally, and ultimately come to a mutual understanding that will provide a path toward a positive and productive resolution.

In addition, be direct and clear with your choice of words. This is why writing out your thoughts or role-playing the scenario in advance can be helpful because it's common, when nervous, to speak too much or "beat around the bush." Therefore, make sure you are speaking clearly and succinctly to avoid confusion and unnecessary banter.

DON'T BEG OR BORROW

While part of being professional and considerate of others requires being mindful of your words, there are two phrases that are not necessarily inappropriate but should be avoided at all costs if void of truth and rationale: "Because I'm the Chair" and "Because that's what the Dean wants."

Although you're human and may pull the chair card out once or twice (i.e., beg them to comply), please try to refrain from doing so. Anytime you simply respond with "Because I'm the Chair" or borrow from your Dean or someone else above you without their consent, you have either lost control of the situation or don't have a sound rationale for making the request. Either way, it reflects poorly on your character and integrity.

For example, Dr. A asks you why she has to complete her annual review differently from previous years, especially when her colleagues in the department and across campus are still doing it the old way. If it's honestly because you and/or the Dean want her to and have a sound reason, then let her know. However, if you can only tell her "That's how the Dean wants it" or "Because I'm the Chair and I said so" you're being inconsiderate and probably dishonest.

Part of being an honest, transparent chair who tells the truth (without saying everything that's true) is providing sound rationale for requests you make of others. This doesn't guarantee that everyone will be happy but still sends the message that you care enough to tell people why you're asking them to do something. Therefore, be careful and neither beg people to comply because you lack rationale nor borrow unauthorized power from those above you. It's not necessary, it causes additional problems and, overall, you're too good of a leader to do this.

AVOID THE COWARD'S COVE

Timing is everything and while the type of conflict-related conversations you will have and with whom (individuals, small, and/or large group) will vary, it all starts with an initial notification. Whether you send an email, make a phone call, or even initiate the request in person, you will almost always know in advance that there's a problem and those with whom you need to speak. Therefore, unless it's a true, unexpected emergency, avoid delivering the initial piece of concerning news and/or scheduling the meeting within the "Coward's Cove" which is:

- Monday through Thursday—before 8:00 a.m. and after 3:30 p.m.
- Friday—before 8:00 a.m. and after 2:00 p.m.
- Anytime on Saturday and Sunday.

As a leader, there are only two reasons to deliver bad news or have the difficult conversation inside of the Coward's Cove:

1. It's an honest, unavoidable emergency.
2. You want to intentionally make the other person sweat and fret.

In addition, be honest when giving a reason for the meeting request. Even though you don't have to explain all of the details, it's still reasonable to say, "We need to talk regarding a few student complaints" instead of "We need to discuss a class-related issue." Above all, avoid the phrase that is the most cowardly of all: "It's a personnel issue."

Be courageous and avoid the Coward's Cove by requesting the conversation and holding the subsequent meeting earlier in the day. Remember the life cycle of a problem. Sending the email at 4:59 p.m. on a Friday or holding the meeting late in the afternoon so the person is forced to leave as soon as it's over will only make things worse. Actually, this causes another problem by assuming the person isn't smart enough to know what you're doing and, as their leader, sends the message that your comfort is more important than theirs, which reveals your true character. You have one chance to request and have the conflict conversation and get it right. One chance to be part of the solution and not part of the problem.

> You have one chance to request and have the conflict conversation and get it right.

NEGOTIATING CONFLICT

After adhering to the guiding principles for conflict communication, which sends the message to the other person that you respect them, want to get it right, will be direct and honest, and will not shy away from the conflict by the day and time it's scheduled, it's time to have the conflict-based conversation. Although chapter 8 offered advice on conflict preparation, the following section is more in-depth and pertinent to the actual application of the conversation, providing a template and rationale for the subsequent dialogue. Chapter 10 will take these principles a step further by providing separate conflict scenarios with supporting dialogue.

Each time you have a difficult conversation with another person or group of people, you are trying to negotiate the problem by coming to an agreeable solution. In the book *Never Split the Difference: Negotiating as If Your Life Depended on It*, former FBI hostage negotiator Christopher Voss provides an excellent and in-depth framework for the art of negotiation. Fortunately, department chairs should never have to take part in a true hostage negotiation. However, the concepts Voss presents are applicable to any type of conflict-based scenario in which the goal is to come to a positive resolution. To effectively prepare for and execute a negotiation or conflict-based conversation, Voss suggests the following steps:[2]

- Identify the goal
- Summarize the situation
- Label their concerns
- Use calibrated questions

Identify the Goal

The first step to any conflict-based conversation is to do your homework and come prepared, having thought about all of the possible outcomes. According to Voss, you should "think through best/worst-case scenarios but only write down a specific goal that represents the best case."[3] In other words, what would be a reasonable, realistic goal, or outcome of the conversation?

Another way to think of this, as mentioned in a previous chapter, is asking about the "one thing that could change everything," with the caveats that it can't include a miracle or violate any university policies or break any laws. While effective in one-on-one conflict conversations, this is especially useful when trying to mitigate conflict between two or more people.

For example, you have confirmed that one of your faculty members, Dr. Z, has been canceling class to the point that the students have complained, stating it's not fair that they have paid tuition, are not learning anything but will still be held accountable for assignments and the final exam. The only rationale that Dr. Z has provided the students is that they're a tenured professor and can cancel class anytime they want. In addition, they have told the students it will better prepare them for graduate school.

In preparation for the conversation with Dr. Z, the main goal could be to get them to stop canceling class so that the students are provided a quality experience. An additional goal could be to get a better understanding of why they feel they have the authority to cancel class without regard for the students' academic success.

Summarize the Situation

In addition to taking time to identify and write down the goal, you should also "summarize and write out in just a couple of sentences the known facts that have led up to the negotiation."[4] This is part of the pre-conversation preparation and forces you to summarize and synthesize the information into a small, manageable piece of information. One way to approach this is to try to summarize the issue in three to five brief sentences that you can share with the other person during the conversation.

In the scenario regarding Dr. Z, the situation could be summarized as follows:

- Six weeks into the semester, Dr. Z has canceled their Tuesday/Thursday class seven times.
- As the chair, you have received five separate emails from students in the class and have had another four students meet with you personally to provide evidence and share their disappointment and concerns.
- Dr. Z has told the students it is their right to cancel class as a tenured professor.

- Dr. Z has told students that, despite the canceled classes, they will still be responsible for the course assignments, including the final exam.
- As the chair, you have confirmed with your Dean, the faculty union representative, and the university attorney that this is unacceptable behavior for a tenured faculty member and, should you choose to pursue it, grounds for disciplinary action.

Label Their Concerns

Labeling the other person's concerns is a way of identifying their feelings, turning them into words, and then very calmly and respectfully repeating their emotions back to them.[5] After sharing your summary of the situation with the other person, Voss suggests preparing three to five labels in order to also perform an accusation audit, which is really another way of saying "I don't want you to feel" and typically phrased as "It probably seems like."[6]

Using labels with an accusation audit addresses the other person's fears and concerns while also disarming them by acknowledging all of the bad things they could say or think about you and the situation. By doing this, you are clearing the path for a more productive conversation in which you can squarely focus on the problem and subsequent solution, without causing more problems.

Voss provides a list of fill-in-the-blank labels that are effective and applicable to almost every situation and can help glean more information from the other person while also defusing any accusations they may have against you:[7]

- It seems like_____is valuable to you.
- It seems like you don't like_____.
- It seems like you value_____.
- It seems like_____makes it easier.
- It seems like you're reluctant to_____.
- It seems like_____is important.
- It seems you are worried that_____.

After you present the summarization of facts to Dr. Z, they're likely to feel attacked and believe that they're entitled to do whatever they want because they're tenured. To be more precise and to enhance the process, here is a list of how Dr. Z may feel along with potential accusations they could make:

- I'm entitled to do whatever I want. I'm tenured and they can't make me do anything.
- If these students are really "college material," they should be able to read the book and complete the assignments and exams on their own. After all,

it's an upper-level course. If they can't do this, then they certainly won't be ready for graduate school.

- I'm actually helping them prepare for graduate school since they will have to be more independent and can't rely on the instructor to spoon-feed them everything.
- The chair doesn't like me and is just out to get me. I know he's trying to promote a new culture of doing the right thing. Probably just a way for him to get the next high-paying job.

This is just a general list but taking the time to anticipate the other person's rationale along with how they may view you as the chair will make the conversation more productive, if the labels are presented correctly. Here are how some of the labels could be used with Dr. Z's situation, starting first with a few accusation audits. Please note you would not have to use or say all of these in the conversation but taking the time to write them out and even role-play with another person beforehand would be useful.

Dr. Z . . .

- It probably seems like I don't care about you and will not be fair. (Accusation Audit)
- It probably seems like I'm just doing this to prove something and pad my CV for the next job. (Accusation Audit)
- It seems like preparing students for graduate school is valuable to you. (Label)
- It seems like you don't like to be burdened with teaching this class as it's scheduled. (Label)
- It seems like you value your personal time, outside of your assigned duties. (Label)
- It seems like canceling class makes your personal life easier. (Label)
- It seems like you're reluctant to come to campus and teach your assigned classes. (Label)
- It seems you are worried that showing up to teach this class infringes on your rights as a tenured professor. (Label)

The desired outcome or response to the accusation audit is that it will oftentimes cause the other person to refute the claim and admit they don't feel that way. For example, when you tell Dr. Z, "It probably seems like I don't care about you and will not be fair," it's likely (and also human nature) they will reply with "No, that's not true."

Likewise, the main goal of the label is to cause the other person to agree, saying, "That's right." According to Voss, "when your adversaries say, 'That's right,' they feel they have assessed what you've said and pronounced it as correct of their own free will. They embrace it."[8] For example, it's possible that when you say, "Dr. Z, it seems like you value your free time," they will respond with "That's right." Through using an accusation audit, you have addressed any elephants in the room in terms of their negative feelings about you and with the labels, you have enabled Dr. Z to agree with you, which is an indicator that they are willing to discuss the situation and be open to solutions.

Use Calibrated Questions

The last step is to use calibrated questions which are those that "begin with *what, how*, or, sometimes, *why*."[9] These calibrated questions naturally create an open-ended question that requires a detailed response and can be an invitation for the other person to share their true thoughts and feelings. Here are common calibrated questions that can be used in almost any conversation:[10]

- What are we trying to accomplish?
- How is this worthwhile?
- What's the core issue here?
- How does that affect things?
- What's the biggest challenge you face?
- How does this fit into what the objective is?
- How am I supposed to do that?

While not included in Voss' list, another effective calibrated question, especially in higher education, is, "What does fixed look like?" or "How can we fix this?" For example, after having disarmed Dr. Z with the accusation audit and getting them to agree that they really value their free time, and felt entitled to cancel classes, you could say:

> Dr. Z, since we've agreed that there's no animosity between us, we both care about the students and while you clearly value your free time, canceling seven out of twelve classes is still unacceptable, even for a tenured professor. What's the core issue here? How can we fix this?

If Dr. Z says the core issue is that they're overwhelmed due to a mixture of personal and professional issues, then that's a starting point to mutually explore a solution. However, if they aren't as agreeable and reply with, "The core issue is that I don't care what people say. As a tenured professor, I should be able to do this and as my chair, it's your job to make it happen," you could use another calibrated question, designed to throw it back to them: "Dr. Z, what you've asked me to do could get me fired. *How am I supposed to do that?*" In the end, the goal should be to get to a place where Dr. Z agrees with your calibrated question, which will open the door to developing a solution.

This framework for negotiating conflict is effective and can be a true life saver for those who are professionally trained in the field, which doesn't include department chairs. Because of this, the good news is that you will not have to engage in such high-stakes, life and death negotiations, even though some faculty may think their world will end if they don't get the office with the big window. The bad news, however, is that your conflict conversations will come in many varieties. Therefore, the following principles can be used to enhance or modify the aforementioned negotiation tactics to address the nuances of conflict in higher education.

RESOLUTION VS. RETRIBUTION

Although it's possible that this notion could come up during a one-on-one conversation in which you are addressing the actions of another person, such as the scenario with Dr. Z, it will almost always need to be addressed when dealing with conflict between two or more people. When an individual feels another person has mistreated them, regardless of the severity or what's really at stake, the afflicted person may want more than a reasonable solution and expect their "pound of flesh." Because of this, it's wise to let the offended individual know up-front that not only will the rules, policies, and protocol of the university will be followed to reach a resolution, but you will neither advocate nor tolerate any type of retribution. Furthermore, make it clear that you will not mistreat or be mean to another person on their behalf.

This may sound a bit harsh but it can happen without the offended person realizing they're asking for retribution instead of a resolution. For example, Dr. Stalwart requests a meeting with you to discuss Dr. S who, despite meeting the minimum expectations for teaching, scholarship, and service, doesn't spend as much time on campus as Dr. Stalwart would like. As a result, Dr. Stalwart thinks it's unfair and sends the wrong message that Dr. S is "allowed" to do this and wants you to punish him by withholding research funding and publicly shaming him with an email to the department, commending those who show up to campus and condemning the one person who "we all know is too important and entitled to come to work."

Honestly, you may share Dr. Stalwart's frustrations but from an administrative standpoint, unless your university, college, or department has a policy quantifying the number of hours a faculty member must be on campus, outside of the expectations in their contract and the promotion and tenure guidelines, doing what Dr. Stalwart suggests could get you a free trip to Human

Resourcesville and might jeopardize your position as the chair. In addition, Dr. S will now be your new, best enemy. Although there are usually resolutions to most problems or ways to brainstorm even the most trivial concerns, it is never appropriate to pursue retribution.

In the unfortunate event that someone does something that violates university policy or even breaks a state or federal law, rest assured it will not only be taken out of your hands and moved to higher administration or external authorities, but the guilty party will receive an appropriate consequence. In any event, it's not your place to impose retributions and be unkind or even harm another person.

GROUP REPRIMANDS

Group reprimands, warnings, and suggestions don't work unless every person receiving the message is at fault. Even then, it's not an effective way to address conflict so don't do it. In fact, doing so oftentimes makes those for whom the message was intended feel as though they are off the hook and that their behavior is normal because there are obviously other people doing the same thing. Warning everyone sends the message to no one. As a courageous leader, address conflict one-on-one in private. Save the group emails for public praise when it's your intention to send the same, positive message to everyone.

Warning everyone sends the message to no one.

ALL'S WELL THAT ENDS DOCUMENTED

For a conflict-based conversation to end well, there must be clearly defined and mutually agreed-upon consequences and expectations. One way to do this is through drafting a Memorandum of Understanding (MOU) which indicates the following:

• The date, time, and location of the conversation.
• A brief description of the purpose of the conversation.
• Items that accurately reflect what was discussed.
• Items that accurately reflect what was decided and the related expectations.
• Items that directly indicate the time frame in which the expectations should be completed and how the person will be supported, most likely by the chair.

- Items that directly indicate what the consequences will be for not meeting the expectations.
- All related parties, usually the chair and at least one other person, sign, and date the document.

It's important to note that unlike a Memorandum of Agreement (MOA), an MOU is not legally binding and is simply a written description of what was discussed and agreed upon and can be used to summarize and document any type of conversation with faculty, staff, and students. In the event that the other person is unwilling to sign an official MOU or if your university doesn't allow them, simply send the other person an email that accurately depicts the conversation, expectations, time frame, and consequences. In the email, give them a deadline to reply, indicating that a nonresponse by the given time will be considered consent. In addition, send the email with a read-receipt attached for additional documentation.

When it's time to officially bring the conversation to a close, let the other person know that while productive, it was understandably a bit uncomfortable. However, they are now in control and their decisions and actions will decide the tone of the next conversation, based upon their adherence to the MOU or related document. Telling them "you decide the next conversation" is not only truthful but also symbolizes the end of the interaction, showing that you do not judge them as a person, all things will stay confidential and their decisions will truly dictate the future. If they adhere to the expectations, you will have positive and comfortable conversations; if they fail to meet expectations, you will have another conversation, more uncomfortable than the first one in which they will have less control over the outcome.

"You decide the next conversation."

FINAL CONSIDERATIONS

Finally, the following list of questions can be useful in establishing a fair and professional mindset when addressing conflict. In fact, this list can be shared with others since it's effective for all parties involved in conflict, regardless of the severity and can further promote a healthy organizational culture.

If you have a conflict or problem with another person, ask yourself the following:

- What's going on in my life that might impact how this affects me and how I view it?
- To what extent is this affected by unmet, unrealistic expectations that I have imposed on myself and others?
- How's my attitude? Do I enjoy my job? Am I pursuing my passion through this work? If not, who is ultimately responsible for my happiness, success, and career trajectory?
- What are some of my blind spots or emotional triggers that may be affected?
- Are my intentions professional, honorable, and reflect my inner qualities, beliefs, and integrity?
- Have I behaved in a way toward others that is not in line with my job duties?
- Have I proactively and professionally visited with the appropriate individuals about this?
- Have I scheduled a mediation visit involving my supervisor or other appropriate individuals?
- Have I made the problem worse through gossip, innuendo, making assumptions, and/or avoidance behavior?
- What does "fixed" or "resolved" look like? Do I want a resolution or retribution? Are these outcomes realistic and a positive reflection of my character? How would I want to be treated in this situation if the roles were reversed?
- How can I be a positive and productive part of the solution and not part of the problem?

In the end, it is possible to become more comfortable with the uncomfortable task of addressing conflict through intentional study and practice. As demonstrated in this chapter as well as chapter 8, one must consider a number of variables, personally and professionally, when confronting conflict. In fact, preparing for one, thirty-minute conflict-based conversation may require at least one hour of preparation. However, time spent in preparation and anticipation of the conversation usually results in a shorter, more positive, and productive interaction. Given the amount of attention that has been given to conflict preparation and execution, the following chapter will pull everything together by presenting conflict scenarios and related dialogues.

Chapter 10

Conflict Scenarios

Practice makes perfect
—Benjamin Franklin

Given the multitude of variables that occur on a college campus and within each academic department, you will be faced with different types of conflict, ranging from one-on-one to mediating a conflict between two or more people or addressing conflict with a large group. While there are some similarities across all difficult conversations, the following will provide insight into the nuances faced by department chairs while applying some of the principles mentioned in previous chapters. Please note that all scenarios are fictional and names will use the pronouns "they" and "them."

SCENARIO A DESCRIPTION

Scenario A provides an example of a typical, one-on-one conflict conversation in which a faculty member has done something and, as the chair, you must address it and, most importantly, take steps to effectively and efficiently resolve the problem.

Dr. A is a second-year, tenure-track faculty member in your department. While they tend to be a very effective instructor and respond well to student needs, they don't work well with other faculty members. Moreover, they routinely argue with you and other upper-level administrators in public meetings and once filed a grievance against a colleague for "not properly acknowledging them in the hallway." In addition to your observations of their behavior, the majority of your faculty members have come to you—individually and in small groups—to complain, saying they refuse to serve on committees with Dr. A and have even threatened to boycott departmental meetings due to their aggressive behavior and need to control the conversation. As the chair, you have also noticed Dr. A's behavior in meetings and have tried to redirect their behavior but it's clear that it's time for a more direct approach.

Scenario A Preparation

As soon as you are made aware of the issue and realize you have to address it directly with Dr. A, go through the pre-conflict checklist.

Seven, Nine, Crime, or Dime?

You have determined that this is not a violation of Title VII or IX, it hasn't violated other policies (isn't a crime) and doesn't involve the inappropriate use of money.

Why Do You Lead and Serve?

Remind yourself that conflict comes with the job and when we let the bad grow, the good will go. If you respect those in your department who are the true "super stars," then you must address this issue with Dr. A. Failure to do so is akin to telling others in the department they don't matter.

Have You Built a Relationship?

How well do you know Dr. A? What are their strengths and areas of interest? Have you had any positive or pleasant interactions? To what extent have you built relational equity with them?

Transpose the Problem

Pick the person in your department or even on the campus that is the least likely to behave like Dr. A in meetings and consider how you would approach this conversation with that person. If you find you would be more kind and forgiving, then extend the same courtesy to Dr. A.

Choose Courage and Extinguish Fear

Remember, leaders earn their money on the difficult days, having conversations that most people would rather avoid. Be the leader your people need and choose courage. In addition, remember that you may very well upset Dr. A and create an enemy. While it's not desirable, if it happens, there's little you can do to control it. In the end, you have covered your bases. The worst thing

Dr. A can do is claim you have poor character by showing their true character through spreading gossip and trying to stir up drama. If that happens, then you will have to have yet another, more uncomfortable conversation with Dr. A.

Prepare

Prepare for the conversation by identifying the goal and summarizing the situation. Also, prepare a few accusation audits, label Dr. A's potential concerns, and prepare calibrated questions. In the end, answer for yourself, "What does fixed look like?"

Avoid the Coward's Cove

It's time to contact Dr. A and request the meeting so do so outside of the Coward's Cove, making sure to provide enough detail so that they are aware and can also adequately prepare. As a reminder, the Coward's Cove is Monday through Thursday (before 8:00 a.m. and after 3:30 p.m.), Friday (before 8:00 a.m. after 2:00 p.m.), and anytime during the weekend

Conflict Scenario A

You send Dr. A the following email at 9:00 a.m. on Monday morning:

> To: dra@univesity.edu
> Subject: Concerns related to behavior in meetings
> Dr. A:
>
> Good morning. I'm writing to request an in person meeting this Wednesday at 1 p.m. in my office. It has been brought to my attention that there are concerns about your behavior in department meetings. Accordingly, I would like to discuss this with you further to see if I can ascertain a better understanding of the situation in hopes that we can come to a reasonable conclusion moving forward.
>
> Please note that this is just a conversation between the two of us and, at this point, I am convinced this will remain at my level and not need to progress any higher.
>
> Sincerely,
> Dr. Chair

Prior to the meeting on Wednesday at 1 p.m., remind yourself that you are there to "be right" and not just "get it right," making sure to address the problem and not Dr. A as a person. In addition, be direct with your intentions and words and don't pull the "Because I'm the Chair" card or borrow from your dean saying, "This is what Dr. Dean wants to do."

Chair: Good afternoon, Dr. A. Thank you for coming in today. Please have a seat. Can our administrative assistant offer you anything to drink?

Dr. A: No thank you. I'm not exactly happy to be here and don't intend to stay long.

Chair: Ok. I also hope to make this an efficient and productive meeting. I know you have your own work to tend to today.

Dr. A, here's where we're at. I think you're a great addition to our department and nobody can question your dedication to your students and your scholarship. However, a significant number of concerns have come my way from our colleagues in which they are upset with your behavior in department meetings. While I cannot share their names, they feel as though your constant interruptions, sarcasm, and negative comments when things don't go your way are out of line. In addition, as the chair, I have also noticed this behavior and have made attempts to correct it. Therefore, the purpose of today's conversation is to better understand what's going on and come up with a plan so it doesn't happen again. I realize this is stressful and uncomfortable and it probably seems like I'm just out to get you.

Dr. A: No. I don't think you're out to get me but it's clear everyone else is. But that's not new because nobody on this campus respects me.

Chair: Nobody? I'm on this campus and I respect you.

Dr. A: Well, you know what I mean. This is probably just two or three people who are jealous.

Chair: It seems like you value other people's opinions of you.

Dr. A: I don't know. I mean, I don't care what most people think but I don't like it when people assume they know me. I'm not from this part of the country so they just don't understand that we're more forceful where I come from.

Chair: So, it seems like maybe developing relationships with your colleagues might help them understand you better?

Dr. A: That's right. But I don't really spend time with any of them since they don't like me.

Chair: Dr. A, here's the deal. I do agree that the frequency and tone of your words needs to change in meetings but I also know you have a lot to offer. We have some great people in this department so it seems like they just want to have a comfortable environment for meetings. Dr. A, what's the core issue here?

Dr. A: The issue is that a few people are trying to sabotage me and they need to keep quiet. Have you talked with them?

Chair: First of all, this conversation is about you and I don't share confidential personnel issues with others. Second of all, let's place the focus back on our conversation. What does fixed look like here? What can we do so your colleagues understand you have a lot to add to our team, especially in meetings? How can I help?

Dr. A: You can start by telling a few people to shut their mouths.

Chair: Again, this is about you. Also, I will not be mean to other people on your behalf, just like I am here today to be professional and kind to you.

Dr. A: Ok. I get it. I know I can be obnoxious at times. I guess I just really want people to know I care and have opinions. Since I started I have always felt like the odd ball.

Chair: I can understand that it can be tough to fit into a department with a lot of tenured faculty who have been here and with each other for a long time. How about this? Each time you are tempted to interrupt in a meeting, I want you to write down what you were going to say or the question you were going to ask. If, at the end of the meeting, you still have these concerns, contact my administrative assistant to set up a meeting with me so we can clarify your misunderstandings. What do you think?

Dr. A: Ok. I guess that will work. Let me warn you, I may have a lot of questions!

Chair: That's fine! I appreciate your willingness to do this. If it's Ok with you, I would like to draw up a bullet-point list of what we discussed today, mainly so I don't forget but also so we are both on the same page. Is this Ok?

Dr. A: I guess. I'm not going to sign anything that is a legal document or will go in my permanent file or promotion and tenure dossier.

Chair: Of course not! This is just between the two of us. I usually like to draft an MOU that looks more official but, in this case, how about I just send you an email outlining our discussion and you simply reply, indicating you received it and understand the expectations? The good news is that if all goes as planned, we'll both forget about it and never look at it again.

Dr. A: That's fine. I can do that.

Chair: Thank you for taking the time to meet with me. I appreciate your cooperation and the great work you do in our department. I want you to know that our conversation today is confidential and in no way affects my opinion of your as an individual, which has always been very positive. I realize this was a less-than-desirable conversation but here's the deal—the ball is in your court. You decide the next conversation. If all goes as planned, we'll continue to have positive interactions, which is what I would prefer. If, however, these issues continue, then, unfortunately, we'll have to have another conversation that won't be very comfortable. Ok?

Dr. A: No. I get it. This won't be an issue any more. I know you're just doing your job and trying to help.

Chair: That's right. I'm glad you understand. I don't want to keep you any longer but, before we end, I just want to make sure you feel as though you were treated fairly today and didn't feel threatened or attacked in any way?

Dr. A: No. I'm a bit embarrassed but I'm fine. You were very kind.

Chair: I also appreciate your professionalism. I've done this long enough to let you know that sometimes people aren't as nice as you have been today! Again, thank you for coming in. I will send the email this afternoon or tomorrow morning. Are we good? Anything else I can help you with today?

Dr. A: No. we're fine. Thanks again.

Chair: Thank you, Dr. A. Enjoy the rest of your day.

SCENARIO B DESCRIPTION

The next scenario involves a conflict of interest or philosophy with Dr. X. While the conversation won't be as uncomfortable as Scenario A, it does provide an overview of how to use the same conflict-negotiation strategies to mediate a conflict of interest with a policy or another individual.

> Dr. B is an Assistant Professor in your department who will be going up for promotion and tenure during the current academic year. While Dr. B isn't outstanding in any of the areas of teaching, service and scholarship, they certainly meet the minimum criteria, as defined by the department and college promotion and tenure guidelines. Therefore, Dr. B will most likely be promoted and tenured, albeit on the lower end of the scale. Dr. X is a full professor in your department and chairs the promotion and tenure committee. By all accounts, Dr. X is an excellent teacher and scholar and is one of the hardest working members of the department. Accordingly, Dr. X is upset because they don't think Dr. B, or anyone with a similar record, should be considered for promotion and tenure. As a result, Dr. X has scheduled a meeting with you to discuss this matter.

Scenario B Preparation

The following is a truncated checklist as some of the personal, philosophical questions addressed in Scenario A would be applicable in this and most every other conflict-based scenario, most notably reflecting on why you lead and serve, transposing the problem and choosing courage, and extinguishing fear and the general, pre-meeting preparation. In addition, it's not necessary to address the Coward's Cove since Dr. X took the initiative to schedule the meeting.

Therefore, there are really two questions to focus on: (1) Seven, nine, crime, or dime? No, this doesn't violate any of these criteria; (2) Have you built a relationship? Yes, you have a very good working relationship with Dr. X.

Conflict Scenario B

Chair: Good morning, Dr. X. I'm glad my assistant was able to get you on my schedule this week. Please have a seat.

Dr. X: Thank you. I appreciate you taking this meeting. I'm just going to get to the point here. As you know, I am chairing our department promotion and tenure committee this year and I really don't think Dr. B should be given promotion and tenure. Nothing against them personally but I've shared these thoughts with you before and nothing happens—they just keep moving forward year after year. I just think it is time to do something because it's an insult to those of us who actually had to work hard to earn the privilege.

Chair: Ok. I will admit that I'm not surprised that this is a concern but my goal.

Dr. X: (interrupting) I'm sorry but something has got to be done. This is the final year and it just seems like Dr. B will slide by like they do with everything else. Remember you always tell us that "We encourage what we tolerate" and need to be courageous leaders. Well, I'm leading the committee, I'm a senior professor so this is me refusing to tolerate mediocrity and taking a stand!

Chair: I can tell you're passionate and probably a bit irritated by this. I want you to feel free to vent and get it off your chest. Do you have more to share or are you willing to hear my thoughts?

Dr. X: Yeah, I'm irritated but go ahead and tell me what you think.

Chair: As you know, my goal is for us to come to some type of agreement or mutual understanding here so that you're comfortable leading the promotion and tenure committee. In addition, since this does significantly affect another person, one of our colleagues, I want us to be clear on how to interpret and apply our departmental P and T criteria in a fair and equitable manner. I know you have shared this concern with me before so it probably seems like I'm just putting you off or unwilling to address this issue.

Dr. X: Yeah, I've shared it but, no, I don't think you're ignoring me. I know you take care of things so that's why I'm here.

Chair: I appreciate your initiative and confidence in me but there are a lot of moving parts here, many of which I cannot control. Overall, it seems like you value the process of earning promotion and tenure?

Dr. X: Of course! I worked hard to earn that privilege here—both times going to Associate and then full Professor. And when I went up, we had some excellent senior faculty who really pushed us to excel and exceed the requirements. I'm not sure half of the people that have gone up the last seven years would have had a chance with the old guard. Unfortunately, most of them have retired. It just seems like we've lowered our standards.

Chair: You and I were first-year "newbies" together so I hear what you're saying about the "old guard." What a great group of people. I know I'm a better scholar for having worked to meet their standards. So, it seems like you're worried that people who haven't worked as hard as others might still receive promotion and tenure and that's not fair?

Dr. X: Exactly! So, you see, you have to do something. You're in the same boat as I am!

Chair: Look, I get what you're saying and I certainly understand that it seems like we have steadily, over the years, lowered our standards. However, I have our Promotion and Tenure Guidelines in front of me and I know you're very familiar with them also. Notice when they were last adopted and approved. It's been awhile. In fact, with the exception of a few minor changes, these are the same criteria you and I were held to. The scholarship criteria haven't changed at all. What are we really trying to accomplish here?

Dr. X: I know the criteria haven't changed but it doesn't matter. It's just not fair, especially to those of us who had to work twice as hard, that Dr. B has made it this far and without you doing something, they will probably receive promotion and tenure.

Chair: And why do you say Dr. B will get promoted and tenured?

Dr. X: Because they meet the minimum criteria, but that's it! You and I had to publish much more and in higher-profile journals. If we would have just met the minimum criteria, they would have sent us packing! You have got to keep Dr. B from getting promotion and tenure.

Chair: And how am I supposed to do that?

Dr. X: I don't know. You're the chair. Talk to the dean or provost. Just make it happen. I'm the committee chair, just tell me to vote "no" and it's a done deal!

Chair: If we came into the office tomorrow and, all of a sudden, this was fixed, what would it take? By the way, no policies or laws can be broken and no miracles can be performed! Seriously, what would have to happen?

Dr. X: Well, ideally, Dr. B would no longer meet the minimum criteria and it would make my job a lot easier.

Chair: Ok. And what would it take for them to not meet the criteria between now and next month when your committee writes the recommendation letter?

Dr. X: You can just determine that Dr. B doesn't meet criteria. I'm sure the Dean will agree.

Chair: That would violate a policy and, in some ways, represent a miracle! Let's be realistic. What would have to happen?

Dr. X: I know—we would have to change the criteria.

Chair: Exactly! And we both know it takes longer than 4 weeks to do it. Heck, we've been talking about changing them for at least 4 years and we're still here with the same document! So, what's the core issue here and how can we move on? It seems like you're upset that some of us had to work harder than others, even though we have all been held to the same standards?

Dr. X: That's right! It just doesn't seem fair.

Chair: I know, but if you were in my position as chair, knowing that meeting the minimum criteria gets one promoted and tenured the same as exceeding them, what would you say? What have you heard me say more than once about this?

Dr. X: I know. We have to follow the guidelines. It's just frustrating.

Chair: I understand your feelings but it sounds like you already know what we can and can't do here and why. We can treat people fairly in this process, even though their promotion and tenure files aren't the same. So, this has taken a bit longer than I had planned but can we agree that, while it's frustrating that some of us worked harder than others, at the end of the day, that was our choice and we have probably reaped the benefits in ways that are outside of just being promoted and tenured?

Dr. X: Yeah, I agree. It's frustrating but I hear what you're saying. We have to apply the guidelines and if we have a problem, when need to change the criteria and can't be unfair to people.

Chair: That's right! I feel comfortable that we have this resolved. Unless you see a need for a formal document, we'll just have a verbal agreement and understanding that although you don't agree with the guidelines, you will apply them fairly. In fact, I think we need to adopt new ones. Since you brought up the idea, you know what that means in higher ed!

Dr. X: I know! Would I like to chair the committee? Actually, I would like to do that if you're Ok with it.

Chair: Certainly. I couldn't think of a better person. How about you pull the tenured faculty together, look at guidelines from across campus as well as those at peer institutions and go from there. Let me know how I can help. I'll stay out of your way but I would like a general outline of the changes by the end of this academic year. Sound fair?

Dr. X: Of course! I'll get on it. Thanks again.

Chair: Thank you for your work and service. We're lucky to have you. Take care and have a great day.

SCENARIO C DESCRIPTION

The final scenario involves conflict that must be addressed individually with a staff member. While there are similarities between faculty and staff-related conflict, there are a few key differences to be aware of, most notably that staff are typically nontenured, "at-will" employees which means they can be terminated for any reason and without warming as long as it is not illegal. Therefore, the stakes and emotions can run a bit higher in these conversations.

Cameron has been an academic advisor in your department for six years and is very passionate and dedicated to their job. In fact, anytime something needs done that will enhance the quality of the advising that students receive, Cameron is the first to volunteer and lead the charge. Although you and Cameron have an established, professional working relationship, there have been a few minor instances in which you have had to tell them that some decisions can only come from the faculty and whether they like it or not, it's the advisor's job to comply. As a result, you have sensed some hostility and perhaps signs of one or more of the "dark triad" of personality disorders. Nonetheless, you have been a consistent, professional and helpful leader to Cameron, remaining above reproach at all times. Unfortunately, the Registrar has just brought it to your attention that after conducting an audit of transfer students' transcripts, they have determined that Cameron has unilaterally and unjustifiably been waiving course requirements and granting transfer credit. The audit determined that this has cost the university hundreds of hours in lost tuition revenue.

Scenario C Preparation

Again, the checklist would be similar in terms of addressing your personal and philosophical principles. Additionally, you have transposed the problem, chosen to be courageous and rationalized any unnecessary fear. Being mindful to avoid the Coward's Cove, you have asked your administrative assistant to email Cameron and request a meeting for Tuesday at 10:00 a.m., indicating that the recent transfer audit has raised questions and concerns about how they have waived courses and granted course transfers.

Finally, you have done your homework by exploring your options with Human Resources and have also notified your Dean of your intentions. Therefore, this doesn't violate any part of "Seven, Nine, Crime or Dime." As previously stated, you do have a working relationship with Cameron but have already had to impose a few consequences and restrictions against them.

Chair: Good morning, Cameron. Thanks for taking the time to visit with me today. Please have a seat.

Cameron: What's this about. Why am I here?

Chair: I'm going to tell you. If you're more comfortable, please sit down.

Cameron: OK. So, what's up? Your assistant said something about a transfer audit.

Chair: Yes, that is correct. Cameron, I want to be very clear here. The information I have been provided is not only accurate but suggests that you have been knowingly, and without anyone else's approval, either waiving courses for some of our transfer students, or providing transfer credit based on courses that do not meet our criteria. This will probably not be a comfortable conversation but I want to let you know up front that I have checked with the appropriate offices, including HR as well as the university attorney and the purpose of this meeting is not to fire you, OK? My goal is to get to the bottom of this by determining why you made these decisions and how we can not only ensure it doesn't happen again but also give you a path of reconciliation. Now, you know I have tremendous respect for your abilities and dedication to our students. At the same time, I know we've had a few disagreements. It probably seems like I'm just here to pile things on you all at once.

Cameron: Wow. Umm, I don't know. I mean, I know this is serious and, I don't know. . . . They're always on us to keep our numbers up and I've been here long enough to know when a student is going to be successful or not and . . . I just wanted to help students. A lot of these transfer students are non-traditional and they really need a degree to get a better job. This actually happens a lot. I have colleagues at other schools that do this all the time.

Chair: This may very well happen elsewhere but right now, we're just talking about you and our university. Also, I realize that you do want to help students succeed. However, you made a bad choice. You are not a bad person—but you did make a bad choice. I have to ask directly, Cameron, and your honesty will affect the outcome today: Did you knowingly waive or transfer classes that you knew were neither a good fit nor approved by the Registrar?

Cameron: Well . . . I really love my job. I love this place. I want to stay here.

Chair: Please answer the question so we can put this behind us.

Cameron: OK, yeah. I mean, yes, I knew what I was doing.

Chair: Thank you. I appreciate your honesty. Now, it seems like you value your job, this university and helping students?

Cameron: Yes! I love being an advisor. I'm just so foolish. I don't know what I was thinking.

Chair: You're not foolish. Don't put yourself down. You made a bad choice, it's OK to have some guilt about this but it isn't worthy of shame—there's a big difference.

Cameron: OK.

Chair: So, here's where we're at. This could have been grounds for being fired but a few us put our heads together and decided we're not going that route. However, I have to ask, what or who empowered you to make these decisions?

Cameron: I don't know. I mean, I have been upset since last year when I didn't think we should add a capstone, research course for our seniors. It just wasn't a good idea.

Chair: I know. And if you recall, we talked about it and came to an understanding.

Cameron: No. Yeah, I remember. I get it. It just really made me mad and I felt disrespected after all I've done for this department.

Chair: Again, as I told you last time, I care too much to ask you to work beyond your job description. You're definitely worth a higher salary but, unfortunately, I would not be doing my job by asking you to do extra duty without offering a raise. OK?

Cameron. Yep. I get it. So, what' s gonna happen?

Chair: Well, in some ways, we've already hashed a lot of this out so moving forward, I am going to ask that you attend a special workshop offered by our Registrar that reviews the ethics and unforeseen consequences of not following protocol for granting credit for coursework. This really could have put us in hot water with our accreditation agency. Anyway, all of this will be confidential but you must do it. OK?

Cameron: OK. I've heard of that training. I'll do it.

Chair: Great. In addition, you will not be allowed to make decisions on incoming courses for at least the next three months. At that time, we'll reassess and go from there. OK?

Cameron: OK.

Chair: Finally, I have prepared this MOU that we, meaning myself along with HR, would like you to sign and date. It will stay between us and we will hopefully never have to look at it again. It simply provides a description of our conversation today along with what we expect you to do as well as the consequences for non-compliance. Feel free to take a copy and get it back to me tomorrow. It's not a legal document but you can have an attorney look at if you wish. Our attorney approved it so they could easily confirm with each other.

Cameron: No. I can sign it. Let me see it.

Chair: Thank you. I will get you a final copy with my signature. OK. Here's the deal. I know this was not comfortable and might be the worst day of your professional life. This isn't fun for me either so let's hope this is it! To be honest, the ball is in your court. Your decisions will determine the tone of the next conversation we have about this, OK? I'm not a fortune teller but I can almost guarantee you if we have to have this conversation again, you may be cleaning out your office instead of signing an MOU when it's over. I don't want that.

Cameron: I get it. Me neither. Don't worry. This won't happen again. I'm embarrassed but thankful you are all willing to help me. I thought I was going to be cleaning out my office today.

Chair: You made a pretty bad decision but you're still a good person. So, to wrap this up . . . do you feel as though I was respectful of you and this situation at all times during this meeting? Did I do or say anything that you found offensive or that caused unnecessary distress?

Cameron: Well, no. I mean, this isn't fun and I feel terrible but it's not you.

Chair: OK. Just know that, as an employee, you have rights and can always contact our Compliance Officer about me or anyone else that you feel has treated you unfairly. It's certainly not my intent but I wanted you to be aware. So, if you don't have any questions, I think we're done here. Again, this is confidential, I'm disappointed but still know you're a great person and are capable of great things in the future. Let me know if you need anything or have questions. OK?

Cameron: Yeah, I will. Thanks. I know we've had our issues but I appreciate it. Have a good day.

Chair: You too. Take care.

Although the three scenarios do not represent all of the possible conflict-related conversations that can and will occur in the life of a university department chair, they do provide a general overview that can be modified and adapted to adequately address other forms of conflict. Preparing for and having these difficult conversations is a skill that can be developed with time and practice, thus making the uncomfortable more comfortable.

Chapter 11

Crisis Leadership

Conflict builds character. Crisis defines it.
—Steven V. Thulon

A crisis is defined as "a state in a sequence of events at which the trend of all future events, especially for better or for worse, is determined."[1] Unlike conflict, crises don't occur on a daily basis in the life of a leader. In addition, crises come in many varieties, ranging from something minor to a once-in-a-lifetime global pandemic. However, if you serve in a leadership role long enough, it's only a matter of time until you will be called upon to effectively lead others through a crisis. Like a lightning bolt, it's difficult to know just when and where a crisis will strike so you owe it to yourself and, most importantly, those you serve to be prepared.

Firefighters never want to see a building on fire, especially with people inside of it. However, when it happens, they trust their training and get to work, knowing that without a doubt, they were made for such a time and circumstance. Similarly, leaders don't hope for a crisis but when they occur, they must come to the forefront, ready to serve others. In fact, a crisis shouldn't change your character and reasons for being a leader but rather confirm and solidify them. In many ways, a crisis is simply an advanced form of conflict.

Therefore, the purpose of this chapter is to present guiding principles that can better prepare you to be an effective leader during a time in which your people will need you the most. In times of crisis, the true leaders within any organization, regardless of their title or job description, will emerge to serve, guide, and comfort others.

Before moving on, it's important to note that any reference to the COVID-19 pandemic is strictly within the context of crisis leadership in higher education and in no way diminishes or denies the fact that the true crisis and tragedy will forever be the millions of lives around the world that were regrettably lost. Furthermore, any mention of seeing the positive aspect to a crisis or using it to enhance an organization is strictly referring to a crisis in general, and in no way suggests leaders or department chairs should be thankful for whatever benefits emerged as a result of the death and devastation of the COVID-19 pandemic. Overall, nobody wants a crisis of any kind and trying to respond positively to help others as their leader neither ignores nor diminishes the significance of the crisis and/or tragedy.

> In times of crisis, the true leaders within any organization, regardless of their title or job description, will emerge to serve, guide, and comfort others.

In March of 2020, college campuses, along with the rest of the world, essentially shut down overnight due to the COVID-19 pandemic. While history shows that leaders in higher education have certainly experienced a variety of tragic, unforeseen crises, it's safe to say that the events of the Spring 2020 semester (in the United States) were of a magnitude that was previously unfathomable. Nonetheless, it was and is possible to better prepare yourself to lead others through a crisis, realizing people have prevailed in the past and will continue to do so in the future. If you're reading this and plan on being a leader in higher education for any length of time, you will have to lead others through some type of a crisis, which could ultimately define you as a leader. Therefore, consider the following guiding principles of crisis leadership:

- Confront and define reality for yourself and others
- Put people first and communicate
- Acknowledge what you know and don't know
- Turn the blacklight into a spotlight

CONFRONT AND DEFINE REALITY
FOR YOURSELF AND OTHERS

As mentioned in a previous chapter, "the first responsibility of a leader is to define reality."[2] During a crisis, you are only human and will naturally feel the effects and related emotions. Take time to process the event and acknowledge your own fears and questions. Talk to your mentors and seek advice. However, as a leader you must also confront and define the new reality for others. Those whom you serve will naturally look to you for guidance, comfort, and assurance. In fact, crisis leadership demands a great deal of humility and vulnerability (i.e., courage). You must be willing to admit that while you don't have all of the answers and certainly cannot predict the future, you are nonetheless confident that, given enough time, you and those you serve will prevail.

The Stockdale Paradox

In *Good to Great: Why Some Companies Make the Leap . . . and Others Don't,* Jim Collins presents the Stockdale Paradox, which he developed after interviewing Admiral Jim Stockdale who was the highest-ranking military officer to be held as a prisoner-of-war in Vietnam. Despite being tortured over twenty times within an eight-year period (1965–1973), Stockdale never lost faith he would survive, while also acknowledging his daily reality.[3] Collins explains the Stockdale Paradox as follows: "Retain faith that you will prevail in the end, regardless of the difficulties. And at the same time confront the most brutal facts of your current reality, whatever they might be."[4]

While it's highly unlikely that, as a department chair, you will ever be faced with a crisis similar to that of Admiral Stockdale's, his experience and Collins' subsequent analysis are still applicable. For example, in March of 2020 when department chairs were faced with the reality that their on-campus classes would have to be moved to some form of virtual instruction, it was impossible to know the duration or final outcome. The brutal facts were that students and faculty were leaving campus and would have to navigate an unknown reality for an unspecified period of time.

Regardless of the severity of a crisis, during the initial wave of shock, people look to leaders for answers. As a department chair, applying the Stockdale Paradox would mean sharing the brutal facts along with unwavering optimism; every crisis has an expiration date. In doing so, you are also defining reality for yourself and those you serve. If there's ever a time to admit that despite not having all of the answers, you still have hope and have everyone's back, it's in the initial phases of a crisis.

Every crisis has an expiration date.

PUT PEOPLE FIRST AND COMMUNICATE

During a crisis, leaders must "keep the main thing the main thing." As a department chair, this involves two important groups of people: your colleagues and your students. A crisis has a way of pruning away extraneous details in people's personal and professional lives, leaving them to simply focus on what's needed to do their job or survive on a daily basis. As a result, you must communicate early and effectively with those you serve, including your own leaders.

In addition to communicating the paradox of not knowing the outcome but, nonetheless, having faith in the end result, realize that leaders set the tone and establish the level of confidence or concern within the organization. The attitude and outlook of those you serve will be a direct reflection of how they see you. In times of crisis, the feelings and actions of an organization are typically in line with that of their leadership.

Communicate Early and Effectively

In the early phases of a crisis, communicate early and often. Start by reminding your department of the guiding principles upon which you will make decisions and share information as this helps reduce anxiety. Even if the situation is changing by the hour and your department isn't immediately aware of the updates, they will be more confident and comfortable knowing your thought process and the parameters in which you will make decisions that will ultimately affect them.

While it's more appropriate to communicate often at the beginning of a crisis, pay attention to the tension and trust your intuition. For example, in the initial weeks after campuses closed due to COVID-19, it was appropriate for department chairs to send daily updates and messages, along with scheduling frequent virtual meetings in order to address concerns and share information. However, as time went on and people became a bit more comfortable, communication could have decreased without jeopardizing its effectiveness. In fact, forcing people to continually meet and/or bombarding them with endless emails beyond the initial phases of a crisis minimize the effectiveness of the message and also implies a lack of trust.

Avoid Toxic Positivity

While it's important to be positive in your demeanor and communication, being brutally honest means doing so even when the truth is negative. Regardless of the facts or context, avoid toxic positivity which is "the belief that no matter how dire or difficult a situation is, people should maintain a positive mindset."[5] It's one thing to display confidence and a positive attitude, it's another to completely ignore and/or diminish people's feelings by sending messages such as "just stay positive!" or "it could always be worse!" According to Dr. Susan David, a best-selling author, Harvard

Medical School psychologist, and one of the world's leading management thinkers:[6]

> Toxic positivity is forced, false positivity. It may sound innocuous on the surface, but when you share something difficult with someone and they insist that you turn it into a positive, what they're really saying is, "My comfort is more important that your reality."[7]

Therefore, as a leader, be mindful of the delicate balance between the need to be positive while also being honest and acknowledging people's feelings. For example, if your office building burned down overnight, a toxic positivity-style response to someone being sad or devastated would be this: "Cheer up and look at the bright side! At least it wasn't your house. Besides, we're all going to get new office furniture now!"

Instead, a more appropriate, truthful, and supportive response would be this: "I know this time is a difficult and tragic time—many of us lost irreplaceable items. Fortunately, no one was hurt. While I know we'll get through this, it doesn't change that fact that we're all pretty shaken up and need to process our emotions."

ACKNOWLEDGE WHAT YOU KNOW AND DON'T KNOW

In times of crisis, it's important to understand and communicate what you know as well as what you don't know. Although it may seem counterintuitive to be able to "know what you don't know," *The Johari Window* can be useful, which is a framework devised in 1955 by Joseph Luft and Harrington Ingham,[8] to help people better understand their relationship with themselves and others and later used by the U.S. government as an analysis technique.

In their framework, Luft and Harrington devised a four-pane window, or matrix, to identify the following areas of perception:[9]

1. The Arena—What is known to one's self and to others
2. Blind Spot—What is not known to one's self but known to others
3. The Façade—What is known to one's self but not known to others
4. The Unknown—What is not known to one's self and not known to others

An adaptation of this framework that can be used for analysis and subsequent communication in times of crisis is as follows:[10]

1. Known Knowns—What do we collectively know at this time?
2. Known Unknown—What do we know we don't know?

3. Unknown Knowns—What do we inherently know but might not realize or be aware of?
4. Unknown Unknowns—What is it that we can neither know nor anticipate?

For example, closures of universities and public schools due to COVID-19 posed a challenge for teacher preparation programs who work to place college students as student teachers in public school classrooms. While virtually all schools and universities were closed to in person learning in the spring of 2020, both colleges and public schools across the United States had different levels of "openness" in the Fall of 2020. As a result, the following is an example of how a university's teacher education department could have assessed the "Known Knowns" and potential consequences of placing student teachers.

Known Knowns

At this time, we know that many public-school districts will refuse to accept college student teachers into their classrooms, even if their schools are partially opened to their own students. In addition, there will be some college students who, despite having access and permission, will have a justifiable reason for not going into a classroom.

Known Unknowns

At this time, we know there will be unforeseen and unintended consequences related to public policy and the health and well-being of all students and related stakeholders. This is further nuanced by the fact that the policy changes in both our university as well as with our public-school partners will affect the student teachers.

Unknown Known

At this time, we know the feeling and consequences of public-school closures from the Spring semester; we don't know the extent to which it will be different (better or worse) in the Fall semester.

Unknown Unknowns

What could happen in the public schools and with our college students that we have not even considered? This would be something that did not occur in the Spring 2020 semester. How can we anticipate, address, and/or avoid these scenarios? To what extent can we ensure maximum control of the unknown variables?

While the preceding scenario is in response to a serious situation, it can also be used with less severe crises. This model, which could be developed collaboratively and also shared with your faculty related to any crisis (hopefully less severe than the one depicted), provides yet another blueprint for decision-making. Furthermore, if the critical question being asked was "Should we place our college students in public schools that are willing to accept them in the Fall semester?", answering the four main areas, in the end, provides a cost-benefit analysis of the best decision along with supporting rationale.

BLACKLIGHT AS A SPOTLIGHT

Just like a conflict, if assessed correctly, a crisis can be used to troubleshoot and enhance an organization. While even the most experienced leaders would prefer to avoid a crisis, when they occur, it essentially shines a blacklight onto the leader and the organization, revealing issues that were present but hidden in plain sight. Even though a crisis can illuminate and reinforce positive aspects of your department's culture, the initial and most effective analysis tends to focus on the less-than-positive fissures and cracks. Therefore, use the blacklight as a spotlight and have the courage and honesty to assess the following aspects that the crisis revealed about your department's culture using the acronym CRISIS:

A crisis reveals our . . .

- **C**haracter
- **R**esilience
- **I**ntegrity
- **S**trength
- **I**diosyncrasies and **I**deals
- **S**elf

Character

If a conflict builds and reveals your true character as a leader, a crisis will define it. Furthermore, this is nonnegotiable—you don't have a choice. Regardless of how you perform on the spectrum spanning from awesome to awful, in the final analysis, how you lead others during a crisis will define your true character and that of the organization for which you are responsible. In addition, a crisis has a way of causing people to either regress or impress, meaning they do what most, normal people do and retreat to their comfort zone or step up and emerge as leaders, regardless of their title and position.

> If a conflict builds and reveals your true character as a leader, a crisis will define it.

Please note that in times of crisis, it's difficult and certainly inappropriate to infer that all people must step up and behave in a certain way because that's not a human nature. In fact, it's more appropriate to assume that most people will initially take a step back and retreat since experiencing the initial wave of a crisis is similar to taking a punch to the stomach. Therefore, the following questions are not meant to judge people's character but, instead, are offered as a means of self-reflection and preparation to help you as a leader and those you will serve in future crises.

- As a leader, what did you do that you are most proud of?
- As a leader, what did you do that surprised you? (Positive or negative)
- As a leader, what would you do differently if you had the chance to do it over?
- What did your leaders (Dean, Provost, etc.) do that you are most proud of?
- What did your leaders do that you wish they would have done differently?
- What can you learn about future crisis leadership from your own leaders?
- Who were the expected and unexpected leaders that stepped up to serve others during the crisis? (Have you been mentoring those people? If not, you may want to start.)
- Overall, how would you describe the character and collective resolve of those in your department?

Resilience

Resilience is defined as "an ability to recover from or adjust easily to misfortune or change."[11] In times of crisis, leaders must have resilience, demonstrating the ability to react and persevere. In addition, there will most likely be individuals in your department who also display a great deal of resilience, being flexible, understanding, and forgiving. The quality of your leadership and the culture you created prior to the crisis will contribute to the overall resiliency of those you serve. Therefore, assess the extent to which your people were able to adapt and adjust and ask how you can either continue to foster that environment or what may need to change to create it.

Integrity

Closely related to character, integrity is defined as an "adherence to moral and ethical principles and soundness of character."[12] A person's integrity is their core foundation. Like a house, if it's solid and on firm ground, the person will be firm and consistent. If the foundation is cracked and unstable, the person will be unreliable, unpredictable, and susceptible to the winds of influence. Therefore, what did the crisis reveal about your foundation as a leader and that of the entire department?

Strength

To reference the adage "bend but don't break," resiliency reveals one's flexibility or adaptability while strength indicates their breaking point or how much pressure they can endure. In fact, strength is defined as the "capacity for exertion or endurance" and the "power of resisting attack."[13] How would you assess your strength as a leader and that of your department? Did you or any of your colleagues reach a breaking point and if so, what was it? Reaching one's limit isn't a sign of weakness as it's oftentimes healthy to take a break, to cry, to vent to a friend, or just feel angry. However, in reflecting upon and assessing your breaking points, could these have been prevented or at least assuaged through improved leadership and/or an enhanced department culture?

In addition, were there any system failures related to your programs and protocol within the department? For example, when COVID-19 forced classes to transition to remote, online learning, how equipped were you to do this? Did this reveal an area of future expansion (assuming it was a strength) or uncover a potential deficit?

Idiosyncrasies

A crisis can test and reveal your idiosyncrasies and ideals, both as a leader and as an organization. An idiosyncrasy is defined as a "characteristic, habit, mannerism or the like, that is peculiar to an individual."[14] Even though they may be considered "quirks" or peculiar, idiosyncrasies are not necessarily negative traits but rather espoused habits and beliefs for which people are neither aware nor able to explain. Consider the habit of meetings, which occupy a large portion of a department chair's agenda.

Even though meetings that typically would have occurred in person were forced online due to COVID-19, do all meetings need to occur face-to-face in the future? Granted, there is undoubtedly an element to in-person meetings that provide a more authentic interaction that it difficult to replicate virtually. However, the peculiar habit or mannerism (i.e., idiosyncrasy) of assuming that each and every meeting, regardless of its purpose and duration, has to take place in person has certainly been challenged by the crisis.

For example, if a group of people need to get together one time to discuss a one-off topic, is the previously assumed notion that it must occur in person still valid? Meeting in person will always be preferable for committees that need to meet multiple times as it's important to understand each other and form relationships, which tends to be more authentic in face-to-face interactions. However, there are also times when, instead of assuming a meeting has to occur in person, conducting it virtually may not only ensure full attendance but may also be a better use of people's time on that particular day.

Ideals

An ideal is defined as a "standard of perfection . . . often taken as a model for imitation."[15] Accordingly, the blacklight of crisis can also illuminate and challenge deep-seated beliefs and overall philosophical assumptions, both personally and corporately. Given the tradition and history of most colleges and universities, ideals can represent the foundation upon which institutions and related departments are founded and continue to operate. Although this is usually one of the many positive aspects to working in higher education, even ideals are subject to an occasional audit.

For example, university closures in March of 2020 forced in-person classes to transition online. When these institutions "opened up" in the Fall semester, many classes remained online while some were converted to a hybrid model in which students attended some class meetings on campus and others virtually, either synchronously or asynchronously. As a result, it's possible that you and your colleagues have questioned what really constitutes a learning experience and how does one define the value of "seat time," given the opportunities to enhance and modify the traditional, in-person classroom experience with technology? This is not to suggest the ideal of in-person instruction is invalid but, instead, simply shows how the crisis may provide opportunities to enhance students' academic experiences through redefining what it means to "be in class."

Self

Finally, in addition to examining your character, resilience, integrity, strength, idiosyncrasies, and ideals, utilize a crisis to reflect upon yourself, both personally and professionally. Give yourself permission to not be perfect because that's not possible when leading yourself and others through a crisis. However, take time to step back and reflect on what the crisis reaffirmed and revealed to you and your organization.

From a professional standpoint, are you still committed to serving as a department chair and perhaps pursuing other administrative roles, such as a deanship? Conversely, has the crisis revealed that your true passion is perhaps going back to the faculty to focus more on your teaching and/or scholarship? To what extent has the crisis changed your view (positively or negatively) of your current institution and higher education in general? Most importantly, focus on what you learned about yourself that you can either change, adopt, or enhance that will benefit you as an individual, regardless of your current profession.

In the end, nobody wants or wishes for any type of crisis, certainly not a global pandemic that shuts the world down. Even so, as a leader, don't neglect the opportunity to learn from a crisis to improve yourself and those you serve.

Chapter 12

The Importance of Hiring

Part I

Quality - most important

People are not your most important asset. The right people are.
—Jim Collins

Organizations and their respective cultures are a result of the people within them along with the quality of their leadership. As a higher education department chair, next to serving students, hiring and supporting great people should be your top priority. Although there are standard hiring practices that must be followed, it can be easy to fall into the trap of thinking that you're "just hiring another position" or even worse, feel forced to hire a position for fear that leaving it vacant may mean it's taken away permanently. Therefore, this chapter will provide an overview of the importance of the hiring process, focusing on appointing the search committee, writing an effective position announcement, collecting application materials, and thoroughly vetting candidates prior to the first interview. The remaining stages of the hiring process will be covered in chapter 13.

Laszlo Bock, former senior vice president of people operations at Google, said, "Hiring is the most important people function you have, and most of us aren't as good at it as we think. Refocusing your resources on hiring better will have a higher return than almost any training program you can develop."[1] The importance and benefit of hiring great people isn't a new concept. In 1914, Edwin G. Booz, an American businessman and cooperate executive, said, "Often the best solution to a management problem is the right person."[2] The culture, vision, mission, productivity, and service of an organization depend on the quality of its people. Therefore, hiring great people is an important process that requires great leadership.

In addition, success breeds success and, over time, great people will tend to attract other great people and affect the quality and success of the entire academic department. This is one of the many reasons it's important to cast a wide net and work to attract and hire from a diverse pool of candidates. The saying "We don't know what we don't know" is applicable here because, in higher education, people can become isolated or siloed into their departments and easily fall into a rut of thinking and behaving the same way. However, universities should still exist to promote unity through diversity among students, faculty, staff, and the communities in which they reside. It's imperative to relentlessly pursue diverse hires who will add value, perspective, experiences, and ways of thinking that will challenge and ultimately improve the department and campus community.

In fact, regardless of the size of the institution or the department, all universities should make a focused, purposeful effort on each and every search to attract diverse candidates, which starts with ensuring the position announcement and subsequent information is not only attractive to all but, most importantly, accurately represents a culture that appreciates and supports diversity, equity, and inclusion.

In an essay titled *Recruiting Diverse and Excellent New Faculty*,[3] Abigail Stewart and Virginia Valian, both of whom hold Distinguished Professorships at their respective universities, offer recommendations for how deans, department chairs, and search committees can increase the chances of attracting and hiring diverse candidates.

To begin, the job description should be written in broad, open terms that are not too limiting and illuminate how the position is flexible with respect to teaching and research. Unless it is a very specialized, specific position, candidates should not immediately be led to believe they're neither qualified nor a good fit solely based on the minimum requirements. In addition, careful attention should be given to make sure the job description isn't written in a way that may be offensive, which can include but is not limited to objectionable or insensitive language.

According to Stewart and Valian, the composition of the search committee is also important because it should reflect the openness of the position as well as the culture of the hiring department and university. Accordingly, committee members should either receive training or already be knowledgeable about diversity, equity, and inclusion as well as the role of implicit bias. A diverse committee will also ensure that a wide range of opinions and viewpoints will be expressed and considered during the interviews and hiring deliberations.

Finally, Stewart and Valian encourage deans and department chairs to publicly acknowledge and even reward departments that successfully hire diverse candidates, which can start with offering new or additional resources to support the search. For example, deans could provide additional funds to support focused marketing or travel to more thoroughly recruit diverse candidates. The committee should also work with the university's Diversity

Officer to ensure they are maximizing their efforts to attract, hire, and retain the best candidates.

THE HIRING PROCESS

Honesty about position when possible

Even though the department chair may not officially serve on the search committee, it's still important to oversee the process, which includes a careful analysis of the open position, writing the job description, appointing the search committee, being a part of the final round of interviews, and contributing to the hiring decision. Consider the following principles as you begin the process.

Fire Before You Hire

Hiring a new position is like adopting someone into your family and shouldn't be taken lightly. You owe it to both your department and the new hire to make sure that there is alignment between the job description, the needs of the department, and the interests, expectations, and experience of the candidate. In short, be honest, transparent, and err on the side of caution and under promise and oversell. For example, don't embellish or augment aspects of the job simply to impress candidates and try to coerce them into taking the job. If there are potential perks you can offer but with limitations, be honest about it. The way candidates are treated during the hiring process says a lot about the true character, culture, and leadership of the department college and university.

Because the potential benefits or consequences of making the right or wrong hire are significant, give yourself and the search committee (once it is formed) permission to fail the search. You will obviously have to run this by your dean, who will hopefully be supportive, but in the end, it's always easier to fire someone before they're hired. Remember, your department's culture is like one big swimming pool that everyone has to swim in. Regardless of the size of the pool or where people are at, it only takes one small drop of a toxic chemical or any undesirable element to ruin the entire environment for everyone.

Although bad hires and toxic individuals can still be addressed "ex post facto" through effective, courageous leadership, it's always better to take a proactive, preventative maintenance approach, and extinguish potential personnel issues before they even sign a contract. It's better to go without the right person than suffer with the wrong one. Therefore, contrary to what some in higher education may think, a failed search isn't the worst possible outcome.

It's better to go without the right person than suffer with the wrong one.

Failing to hire the best candidate can oftentimes be an indicator of a committee, a chair, and a department committed to excellence and unwilling to compromise by hiring a compromised candidate. In addition, while a failed search may be a temporary inconvenience, it sends the message to existing faculty that your culture, standards, and expectations matter and you're committed to finding the best person to join the department.

Waste Not, Want Not

Every person in the department matters which means every open position matters. Never waste an open position or "line," as they are often referred to in higher education. Even if it seems logical that you will hire the same line and job description held by the outgoing faculty member, analyze the big picture in terms of the current and future needs of the department, which also includes being mindful of the current faculty's goals. This is one of the many reasons it pays to know your people and your roster.

For example, after an award-winning career, Dr. Excellent is set to retire and, at first, it appears only logical to hire another "Dr. Excellent" in terms of the classes they will teach and their contributing area of expertise. While it's clear there will never be another Dr. Excellent, as the chair, you do need to fill their classes and other responsibilities for the upcoming academic year. You should always check with your Dean to make sure you have the authority to go forward with a search. However, assuming you are given permission to rehire, the following questions can help reveal other possibilities and ways to reimagine an open position.

- How does this hire support and align with the strategic goals and plan of the department, college and university?
- Given the potential costs savings of an open line, does it need to be rehired and if so, at what level (instructor, assistant, associate, or professor)?
- Are there other positions or initiatives you could support with the extra revenue?
- If the resignation or retirement is too late to run a full-search, can you hire a one-year appointment? If so, will that person have to go through the hiring process when the search begins should they want to apply?
- Are you able to hire or consider a non-tenure, teaching or "professor of practice" line versus a traditional tenure line?

- Is there anyone in the department who is capable and interested in assuming all or some of the responsibilities? In other words, is there room or slack in other places that would enable you to cover this position without a new hire?
- Is there anyone in the department who you think is capable of some of the responsibilities but may not realize it or may need additional training?
- Are there any departmental initiatives that could be supported by altering this position?
- Looking at your roster, do you foresee or know of any upcoming resignations or retirements that may also affect how your hire this line?
- How could the new line contribute to the balance of teaching and scholarship within the department?
- Given the overall profile of your department, how could you reimagine this position to make it more attractive to diverse candidates?

Even though it's possible that you may rehire the open position "as is," taking the time to go through these questions will confirm that you are making the right choice for the right reasons.

The Search Committee

After you have determined that you will rehire the position along with a general framework for the job description and profile, the next step is to put together the search committee. Every step of the hiring process matters and this is no exception. The hiring committee reflects the culture, attitude, and values of the department and university to potential candidates. In fact, this is every bit as important as the style and location of the actual job announcement. It's admirable to catch a candidate's attention with a well-written job posting but it's useless unless the people behind it are equally inviting, engaging, and supportive.

The first person to appoint to the committee is the search chair. Although some departments may have rules (unofficial or official) for who can chair a search, here's a simple two-question litmus test: (1) Can you trust this person to professionally represent the department, college and university in your absence? and (2) can this person professionally and efficiently mediate conflict within the committee? Identifying a person who meets these two criteria will almost always result in an effectively led committee.

After identifying the search committee chair, schedule a meeting with your Diversity Officer (or the relevant office or position on your campus) to ensure you are following best practice for assembling a qualified and diverse committee. While you will naturally need faculty from within the department, it is also wise to consider appointing a few people from different departments in and outside of your own college. Meeting with your Diversity Officer will also enable you to better identify those who have experience and/or relevant diversity training.

Once you and the search chair have formed the committee, schedule a meeting with the appropriate representative from your Human Resources Office to go over the "do's" and "don'ts" of hiring and to also familiarize everyone with any procedures that are specific to the university such as the portal used to collect applications and any required templates. In addition to or concurrently with the HR representative, ask the Diversity Officer to address the entire committee, giving an overview of any relevant policies and considerations, especially with respect to avoiding offensive or hurtful language in the job description and subsequent interviews.

The Job Description

Most universities have a standard template for writing job descriptions or announcements that include minimum qualifications, desired qualifications, information about the department, college, university, and community along with requesting certain application materials. Even though there are elements you cannot control, it's still possible to write the description so that it accurately reflects the department and highlights the flexibility and openness of the position.

The first step in writing the job description is to schedule a meeting with the search committee chair to share your vision for the position and the type of candidate you would like to attract. In fact, make it a point to identify the "can't get" candidate because you assume they would have better offers than yours and write the description to fit them anyway. Please note, this is not to suggest that you profile in a negative way and identify a person you know but instead, you take into consideration all of the variables, including skill set, qualifications, experiences, and diversity and regardless of what you think the odds are, go after that type of person. When it comes to hiring, you can't get what you don't ask for so be bold and write it (don't think it) into existence.

When identifying the "can't get" candidate, don't fall into the trap of assuming they wouldn't come to your university or, if they did, they wouldn't stay long. It's better to surround yourself with those who are good enough to go elsewhere but, because of the people and culture you've built, choose to be a part of your organization. In an article titled *The Secret to Hiring an Amazing Employee Requires Doing Something Most Leaders Aren't*, Laura Garnett suggests that the secret to attracting the best candidates is a willingness to also let them go if and when a better opportunity comes along. Garnett provides the following reasons:[4]

- Millennial employees are already leaving jobs at a higher rate than employees from earlier generations.

- You'll benefit from the continuous wave of fresh ideas.
- Your organization can become known as a stepping stone to better opportunities.

Depending on the size and profile of your department and university, don't hastily assume you can't attract top candidates. Give yourself, as a leader, and those in your department credit for the culture you have created together because it matters. A survey of more than 1,500 workers in the United States and Canada found that "more than one-third of workers in the U.S. (35 percent) and Canada (40 percent) wouldn't accept a job that was a perfect match if the corporate culture clashed."[5] Not only are you hiring a new family member and colleague but candidates are also looking for a supportive and welcoming professional home. Be courageous and go after the best candidate.

The next step is to meet with the entire committee and share your thoughts on the overall job description and the type of candidate you would like to pursue. This includes providing a rationale for going after the best candidate, regardless of how long they may or may not stay in the position. Once again, go through the process of refining the job description and position announcement so it reflects the opinions of the entire committee.

For example, candidates will most likely need a terminal degree but what type of degrees or areas of study can you accept? In addition, will you specifically state that the degree must come from a certain type of institution, such as one with regional accreditation? What about degrees earned in foreign countries? (You will most likely have to get administrative approval to hire those without permission to work in the United States because it may require the university to pay for and sponsor the appropriate visa.). These are common questions that need to be addressed prior to writing and posting the job description.

Another common consideration is the previous experience and accomplishments candidates must have, such as scholarship. While the needs of each search will vary and, to some degree, may be dictated by upper administration, hire for character and talent first and credentials second. This isn't to say that some candidates will get a pass because they all must meet the minimum criteria. However, you can train someone with a terminal degree how to perform job-related skills, provide mentoring, and build them up but you can't give them character or talent.

Hire for character and talent first and credentials second.

Application Materials and Procedure

Although there are more steps, policies, and procedures you may have to address, once you have formed the search committee, understand the hiring protocol and have developed the job description and related announcement, the final step is to determine the application materials you would like candidates to submit. Typically, this involves a cover letter and a CV along with other documents such as a publication or writing sample, a philosophy of teaching and/or a statement related to diversity, equity, and inclusion. Whatever the committee decides to collect, be able to justify it and make sure that each document is thoroughly analyzed, which includes equitable, documented evaluation.

"All's well that ends documented" is not only relevant to conflict conversations but also to the hiring process. Let committee members know that everything they produce, even informal notes, should be saved and will be turned into Human Resources at the conclusion of the search. In addition, clearly define the criteria and evaluations used to determine candidates' progression through each level of consideration. For example, only candidates who (1) meet minimum/required criteria and (2) submit the required materials should advance to the initial round of consideration.

In subsequent rounds of consideration, use the required and preferred qualifications to create a scoring rubric for each category. For example, years of experience or publications could be worth a certain number of points. However, this is not to unfairly exclude inexperienced candidates (remember character over credentials) but simply serves as a tool to initially sort candidates in a way that is consistent. If, at any point in the process, there are questions, always contact Human Resources and request that the inquiry be documented.

Do Your Homework

As the chair of the department, you will most likely have access to the applications as they come in but may not be an active part of the committee until they are ready to identify and conduct first-round interviews, which typically occur using an online platform. However, take the time to train the entire committee, including the chair, how to thoroughly analyze and vet the application materials, especially the CVs since, unfortunately, applicants can be dishonest.

In a study titled *Assessing Trustworthiness in Research: A Pilot Study on CV Verification*,[6] the authors randomly selected 10 percent of the job applicants' CVs submitted to a large research university over a one-year period to verify the accuracy and legitimacy of their research accomplishments.

Focused on applicants within the health sciences, the authors waited 18 to 30 months to verify the accuracy of publications listed as forthcoming. Of the 180 CVs that were analyzed, 141 (78 percent) listed at least one publication and over half of those (56 percent) were determined to be inaccurate. Overall, a total of 193 publications were unable to be verified or were found to be false, which included the following:[7]

- Six articles listed in nonexistent journals
- Seventy-two articles could not be found in journals that did exist
- Thirty-one books and book chapters that could not be verified or did not exist
- Twenty-four forthcoming articles listed in journals that could not be found
- Four instances of "authorship insertion" in which applicants listed themselves on publications to which they did not contribute
- Twenty-seven instances of "authorship promotion" in which applicants falsely listed themselves as a lead author instead of a coauthor or placed their name closer to the lead author in cases of three or more authors
- Twenty-seven instances of "authorship omission" where applicants left other authors off of the publication

The authors of the study offered three hypotheses to account for the large number of unverified or inaccurate publications: (1) an honest error resulting from poor communication among authors related to order of authorship; (2) applicants are intentionally lying because they need a job; and (3) because "some scientists are psychopaths" and "some academics are liars, who lie well, frequently, without hesitation, without regret, and seemingly without getting caught."[8]

The final hypothesis points to the many dangers of not being aware of the "dark triad" of personality disorders (narcissism, Machiavellianism, psychopathy), which can truly destroy a department, a college, and even a university. Perhaps Howard Schultz, who served as the chairman and chief executive officer (CEO) of the Starbucks Coffee Company from 1986 to 2000, and then again from 2008 to 2017, summed it up best when we said, "Hiring people is an art, not a science, and resumes can't tell you whether someone will fit into a company's culture."[9] An addendum to Schultz's comment is that one cannot assume that a resume or CV is always accurate.

Therefore, give the hiring committee permission to be skeptical and thoroughly vet the application materials, especially the CVs, for accuracy in reporting research along with looking for other information and trends that can provide additional insight into a person's true character. For example, try to identify any gaps in employment or education that are not accounted for and acknowledged in the cover letter.

Furthermore, is there a pattern in which the applicant cannot hold a job for more than three to four years at a time? There are always extenuating circumstances but these should be addressed in the application materials. For example, an applicant who appears to be a "job hopper" could share in their cover letter that they have had to relocate for reasons such as a partner's career. (Never ask a candidate about anything related to their personal life, including but not limited to their race or ethnicity, marital status, if they have children, or anything about sexual, political, or religious affiliations and/or preferences.)

Another potential red flag, especially within higher education, is if they are currently on the fourth or fifth year of a tenure-track appointment and have decided to go on the market. There are always legitimate reasons but if this occurs without an explanation, go online and search for their current institution's promotion and tenure guidelines and, based on their CV, look for any glaring issues. For example, if their current department requires a minimum number of peer-reviewed publications by the third or fourth year and they have failed to publish, that might be an indication. By itself, this isn't necessarily a bad sign since they could be coming from a research-intensive school to a smaller one but still, it should be analyzed and discussed among the committee.

In fact, one reason a candidate may be leaving a tenure-track job is due to poor leadership. Even though this can be difficult to completely determine, one strategy is to look at the job openings at the candidate's current institution. Are there patterns related to their department or college? If the candidate has spent many years at their current institution, were they recently passed over for an internal promotion? Were there any new administrative appointments in their college or department for which they were qualified? Finally, has there been a new president or provost appointed within the last year that may also be a contributing factor?

In addition to identifying gaps in an applicant's background, a simple Internet search can reveal the legitimacy of the applicant's places of employment. You should never violate hiring policy and call an applicant's references without their permission, or make any inquires on their behalf. However, in the age of Google and social media accounts, it's not hard to determine someone's background, their associations, and the legitimacy of the claims they make on the job application. In fact, many individuals in higher education are using social media to their benefit, promoting their professional accomplishments and networks. While this can be helpful, the legitimacy of these claims should also be explored.

Vet Yourself

In athletics, it's common for teams to scout their opponents, looking for tendencies that may give them a competitive advantage. In addition, teams will also perform a "self-scout" in which they scout themselves as their opponents would, which can provide an honest perspective of their own strengths and weaknesses and insight into how they are viewed by others. Search committees should do the same and scout or vet themselves as a department, college, university, and community to see how they appear to potential candidates.

For example, committee members as well as trusted colleagues from other campuses should spend some time searching the webpages of the department, college, and university. If you were an applicant with no prior knowledge of the institution or community, what would you think, especially if your background was different than that of the majority of the population? How does the job description appear? Does it send an open and inviting message or is it too limiting? Overall, explore and vet whatever public, accessible resources are available to potential applicants to get a different perspective on how the job, department, and university appear and are portrayed to others.

Hiring great people takes great effort and leadership. Although it's preferable to be able to rehire a position once it becomes available, take the 30,000 feet view and thoroughly analyze the best use of the new position, being mindful of the people, programs, and possibilities within your department. In addition, be purposeful about the selection of the search committee chair and committee members, ensuring that they accurately represent the diversity, flexibility, and openness of the position and the greater campus community. Be diligent and thorough in vetting candidates, which includes looking for gaps, inconsistencies, inaccuracies, or even falsifications. Furthermore, take the extra step of vetting yourself to make sure your department and university are attractive to a diverse group of applicants.

Chapter 13

The Importance of Hiring

Part II

The secret of my success is that we have gone to exceptional lengths to hire the best people in the world.

—Steve Jobs

Hiring great people takes great effort and, like an iceberg, only a small part of the effort is visible to the public. The majority of the hiring process occurs behind the scenes and must be accomplished before the first interview. Chapter 12 discussed the first part of the process, including how to assemble a diverse committee and prepare an effective job announcement, the types of documents required as part of the application process, and how to vet applicants' materials. This chapter will provide the second part of the hiring process, which includes writing effective interview questions, conducting interviews, and making an offer. In addition, the importance of effectively onboarding new faculty will be addressed as well as how to lead faculty when they decide to move on.

GREAT QUESTIONS REVEAL GREAT CANDIDATES

Laura Garnett is a performance strategist who has worked with CEOs from Fortune 500 companies, helping them identify their true potential so they can also inspire those they lead.[1] In her article "The 4 Interview Questions That Will Help You Hire the Right People, Every Single Time," Garnett emphasizes the importance of asking great questions that cannot be found on the application materials and instead, focus on the candidate's motivation, character, and fit, stating that "interviewers should focus on one thing that won't change: who the candidate is as a person."[2] Garnett goes on to share four interview questions that can reveal character, organizational fit, and overall motivation to do the job:[3]

1. What's the thinking or problem solving that you're best at?
2. What's the impact in the world or on others that provides you with fulfillment?
3. Do you see this role as a good fit for who you are and what you need in order to be engaged?
4. What are your values, and what kind of culture is a great fit for you?

These four questions are applicable to higher education and, according to Garnett, will help search committees determine if an applicant is "self-aware, if they'll be truly challenged and fulfilled, and if they'll fit in with the culture of your company."[4]

After thoroughly vetting application materials and using approved, evaluation criteria, the committee should select a group of candidates for a first-round, virtual interview. The total number of candidates can vary based on the protocol of the university and/or the wishes of the Dean. Regardless of the number of first-round candidates, the committee should also develop a list of interview questions that, if robust, can be used during each round of interviews. While it's easy to use common, traditional questions, the answers can frequently be found on the application materials. Therefore, focus on asking great questions that can provide further insight into the following areas: Character, Motivation, Collegiality, and Fit.

Character

While there are many people who would meet the minimum job requirements if they applied, what makes someone a great hire is their character. The interesting thing about searches is that, because of the application process and required materials, they focus almost exclusively on credentials. However, all things being equal among a group of candidates, skills can be taught but character cannot.

As a chair, you will rarely have an uncomfortable conversation or conflict about someone's credentials.

In his best-selling book *Good to Great: Why Some Companies Make the Leap . . . and Others Don't*, Jim Collins studied the habits and traits of some of the world's most successful companies and found that "in determining 'the right people,' the good-to-great companies placed greater weight on character attributes than on specific educational background, practical skills, specialized knowledge, or work experience."[5] Certainly, credentials are important, but great companies and organizations don't hire credentials, they hire character. As a chair, you will rarely have an uncomfortable conversation or conflict about someone's credentials. In the event you have to reprimand or dismiss someone, it will most likely be due to their character. Character outweighs credentials so avoid asking interview questions that have already been answered by the application materials such as "Tell us about your research" or "Why do you want this job?" The following are examples of character-based interview questions:

- Who are some of your role models and mentors and why?
- How do you define leadership? What type of leader do you prefer to work with?
- When have you been the most satisfied and content professionally? Why?
- Tell us about a project or accomplishment that you consider to be one of the most significant in your career?
- To what extent are you willing to take on tasks that are not specifically stated in the job description?
- What would your references say about you if we called them today?
- What are some of your talents and/or attributes that, if hired, you hope to incorporate into this position?
- What are some of your talents and/or attributes that have been overlooked, unappreciated, or underutilized in previous positions?
- *"We are what we repeatedly do. Therefore, success is a habit, not an act"* Based on this saying and professionally speaking, what do you do on a daily basis that has contributed to your success as a teacher and a scholar?

These questions can reveal a candidate's character by focusing on areas such as whether or not they have mentors, which indicates if they're teachable, or what they think their references would say about them, which provides insight into the quality of relationships they have built with those whom they believe will say positive things about them. In addition, other questions can elicit areas in which they feel they are talented and, at the same time, if those have ever been ignored or overlooked at previous positions.

Motivation

Although it might seem logical that an applicant would be adequately motivated for the job, that isn't always true or they may be motivated for the wrong reasons. For example, while it's undeniable that most people need a job to pay the bills, some applicants will cast a wide net, applying for anything and everything without having much knowledge of the institution, including its geographic location. In addition, others, especially those coming directly out of graduate school, may have unrealistic expectations about the salary, benefits, and overall "startup' package the institution can realistically offer.

Finally, some candidates (by choice or by force) have prioritized their location over their vocation and cast a single line rather than a wide net. Instead of going on the market and sending out multiple applications, they only want to apply and work at one institution, which is usually close to where they live. Consequently, this type of place-bound candidate may not be as motivated to establish a research agenda, focus on quality teaching and serve at the national and state levels within their profession, thus indicating they may not be successful on the tenure track.

The following interview questions can be used to reveal a candidate's true motivation for the job and, subsequently, how successful they might be in the position.

- Other than pay, basic health insurance and retirement, what other benefits associated with this position, if taken away, would be a deal breaker? In other words, you would no longer be interested in the position.
- All things being equal (pay, benefits, etc.), if you could have this same position anywhere else in the United States, where would it be and why?
- Finish this statement: If I accept this job, in five years, I will be_____.
- Which of the following factors would be the top two reasons you would accept this job, if offered: (a) the university; (b) the geographic location; (c) the opportunity to do the job, which includes teaching, research, and service; or (d) the people you would be working with?
- Other than the position for which you are applying, what's your dream job and why?

Although it's not a robust list, these questions can help determine the candidate's true motivation for the position. Even though the salary and benefits are a significant factor, there should be other reasons a candidate is motivated to work for the department and university. For example, if a candidate is only applying for the benefits or simply because they're place-bound and feel like they have no other options, it's reasonable to question their motivation.

Collegiality and Fit

Collegiality is defined as "The cooperative relationships of colleagues"[6] and is an essential component to the success of individuals, an academic department, and the entire campus community. While some in higher education may be reluctant to acknowledge and enforce collegiality, "the courts have continued to uphold the use of collegiality as a factor in tenure and other personnel decisions,"[7] essentially making it a fourth component to teaching, scholarship, and service.

Clearly, the extent to which a colleague is cooperative, professional, and pleasant to be around is important. An uncivil colleague is like a toxic chemical being put into the communal swimming pool; it affects everyone and, unfortunately, is common. In a survey of 528 department chairs, 440 (83 percent) responded affirmatively to being asked, "Have you ever had an uncivil or non-collegial faculty member in your department?"[8] The collegiality and overall fit of the applicants (i.e., potential colleagues) are important and should also be addressed in the interviews. The following are examples of interview questions that can provide insight into whether or not a candidate will be a good colleague and fit for the position.

- How do you define collegiality and why is it important in higher education?
- Have you ever worked with an uncivil or non-collegial colleague? If so, how did you deal with that person?
- What if, within a year of accepting this job, you come to realize you're unhappy and it wasn't the right decision. Hypothetically speaking, what would be the main reasons for your unhappiness and regret?
- While maintaining professionalism and confidentiality, tell us about one of the best and worst bosses you've had and what made them this way.
- Think about your previous jobs and complete this statement: My best job would have been better if_____. My worst job would have been better if_____.
- When working with others, what are some behaviors, attitudes, or characteristics that you prefer and work well with?
- When working with others, what are some behaviors, attitudes, or characteristics that you dislike and don't work well with?
- How do you go about building and maintaining working relationships with colleagues, especially those with whom you may not agree?

These questions can help identify how applicants view themselves and others, especially those with whom they may disagree or have conflicts. In addition, asking candidates to predict what factors might cause them to regret the decision to take the position or be unhappy within a year requires them to think about "deal breakers." For example, a candidate's response of "I would be unhappy if I were asked to compromise my integrity and/or knowingly do what's not in the best interest of students" is not as concerning as saying, "I would only regret taking this job if I found out, once again, nobody appreciates me and they are too ignorant to accept my brilliance."

The types of questions that the committee asks should (1) seek to reveal character, motivation, collegiality, and fit and (2) share and reflect the department's culture in terms of values, expectations, flexibility, and openness. In fact, one way to approach writing interview questions is to turn the mission, values, and goals of the department into statements, which can then be turned into questions.

For example, the statement "In Department X, we value civility and collegiality" could be turned into "In what ways would you model civility and collegiality as a member of our department?" Additionally, a search committee can communicate specific expectations through questions such as "We value professionalism in our department and have collegiality as part of our promotion and tenure guidelines. Please share your thoughts about using collegiality as a promotion and tenure criterion."

THE INTERVIEW PROCESS

Although there are similarities across most universities for interviewing candidates, such as conducting the first round virtually and the second round on campus, the intent of this section is to offer general considerations, as opposed to suggesting a fixed protocol. As previously mentioned, the interviews represent the tip of the hiring iceberg and while they are as important as they are public, most of the search committee's work will have already been completed or will take place privately at the conclusion of the interviews.

Whether it's virtual or in-person, it's imperative that the search committee be professional and consistent at every stage of the process, which includes thorough documentation. For example, one set of questions should be developed for each round of interviews to ensure consistency among candidates. Furthermore, the same committee members should ask the same questions in each round of interviews (i.e., Dr. Smith asks question #1 to each of the three candidates in the first round). Once again, an instrument should be developed to fairly evaluate each candidate, using criteria that reflect that requirements of the position. Although, as the department chair, you may not be on the hiring committee, stay in contact with the search chair so you can adequately prepare for the on-campus interviews.

After selecting the finalists to interview on campus, consistency is important. As with the job description, there is usually a standard agenda used to ensure candidates can visit with the same individuals such as the committee, department chair, dean, and Human Resources. This can vary by institution so start with the standard, required agenda.

In addition, be mindful of the fact that while everyone with whom the candidate interacts should be authentic, how candidates are treated during the interview and subsequent onboarding process sends a powerful message. The way people are treated as visitors is an indicator of how they'll be treated as residents.

Chair Questions

Depending upon the protocol and policies of your university, at some point, you will have the opportunity to interview the candidates one-on-one, typically while they are on campus. One of the many benefits of taking the time to recruit and develop effective search committees is that you won't need to replicate any of their questions since you will have access to the answers; however, you can still ask similar questions for clarification.

> It's easier to have a difficult conversation with a faculty member before they're a member of the faculty.

Therefore, use your time with the candidates to further determine if they will be a good fit for your department while also promoting your expectations, vision, and culture. It's always easier to "fire before you hire" and likewise, it's easier to have a difficult conversation with a faculty member before they're a member of the faculty. Obviously, avoid asking questions that are inappropriate or sensitive and always let candidates know they are free to decline to respond to any of your questions. The following are examples of questions you could ask candidates as the department chair. Please note you may only want to select a few of these to be considerate of time, allowing the candidate to ask you some of their own questions.

- In what areas are you naturally intuitive?
- Up to this point in your career, what are you most proud of and why?
- We've all had good and bad bosses or leaders. In a perfect world, describe your ideal department chair. This is your opportunity to directly tell me what kind of leader you would expect me to be if you were hired for this position.
- Who are the top three researchers in your field right now?
- What are the current topics being researched and/or debated in your field?
- It's been said that "everyone has one change-the-world speech in them" or to take the pressure off, at least one good Ted Talk. If I gave you twenty

minutes to prepare to give this presentation to our faculty today, what would you talk about and why?
- What do you hope to accomplish professionally within the next five years? What do you ultimately hope to accomplish in your career?
- How do you feel about being given mastery, purpose, and autonomy while also being held accountable to expectations?
- Let's say that you're convinced beyond a shadow of a doubt that you have the best idea in the department for a new program. It might be the best idea the university has seen in a decade. How would you respond to being told "no," realizing it's not going to happen?
- As a faculty member, how do you define transparency?
- As a faculty member, how do you define shared governance?
- What are at least three questions you have for me?

Checking References

Another important task that can occur at various stages of the hiring process is checking references. For example, some committees may be directed to contact references for finalists prior to their campus visit while others may only contact the references for the top candidate. In any event, still maintain professionalism and consistency by asking each reference the same questions, making sure to document their answers. Also, and perhaps most importantly, only contact references that the candidate has listed, thus providing their consent.

While it can be tempting to call a "friend of a friend who used to work at the candidate's university," it's both unnecessary and highly unethical. What message does it send to the candidate? They have met or exceeded all of the criteria from the application process through the final interview and, despite what you may have told them about your own integrity you still don't trust them. Therefore, you knowingly violated protocol and policy to go behind their back and check off-references, assuming that they surely couldn't be as good as they appeared. Granted, anything the candidate shares publicly online is fair game but checking off-references is unethical. Remember, a candidate is also interviewing the department and university so be mindful of the messages you send.

Selecting a Candidate

Of all the processes associated with hiring a new colleague, the protocols and policies associated with how to select a candidate and ultimately make the offer can be significantly different among each institution. While you should always check with your Dean and Human Resources to ensure compliance, here are a few examples of how committees may select the final candidate(s):

- The committee has the authority to select the person whom they want to hire.
- The committee has the authority to recommend (to the chair and/or Dean) whom they want to hire.
- The committee is asked to rank their top three finalists, which are then sent to the chair and dean.
- The committee is asked to provide an unranked list of their top three finalists, along with documentation of the strengths and weakness of each candidate, which is then shared with the chair and dean.

It is helpful to know the expectations for selecting or recommending the final candidate prior to beginning the deliberation process. As the department chair, you may also have some flexibility in terms of how involved you are with the committee's discussions and final suggestions. If possible, schedule a meeting with the committee chair to share notes and revisit the initial goals of the search. Next, meet with the entire committee to gather their input about the best hire, based upon all of the collected materials and observations. Keep in mind that failing a search is not the worst possible outcome.

Assuming that a final candidate is identified, the policies of each institution will determine how the official offer and subsequent negotiations are handled. If, as the chair, you are a part of the offer or can visit with the finalist to answer questions, remember that every interaction matters and you're building a relationship and accumulating relational equity before they accept the job and come to campus. In addition, be honest and accommodating but also set boundaries. The way you treat someone coming in establishes the long-term parameters and expectations of your relationship. For example, don't promise what you can't deliver or offer incentives or "treats" simply to coerce the candidate to take the job, especially if you would not be able to offer the same benefits to other potential hires coming into the department.

ONBOARDING

It may be tempting to think that once the candidate has accepted the job and has officially become a new colleague, the hiring process is over. While much of the paperwork and protocol related to Human Resources is finished, the final step of the hiring process, onboarding, is just beginning.

Onboarding can be defined as "the systematic and comprehensive approach to integrating a new employee with a company and its culture, as well as getting the new employee the tools and information needed to become a productive member of the team."[9] The onboarding process not only supports new hires, welcoming them into the culture of the organization, but also contributes to their longevity, as onboarded employees are 58 percent more likely to stay with the organization after three years.[10] Additionally, retaining great people is financially wise since replacing an employee can cost as much as 33 percent of their annual salary.[11]

The Corporate Leadership Council (CLC) surveyed more than 50,000 employees from fifty-nine organizations, thirty countries, and fourteen industries to determine engagement strategies, such as onboarding, that lead to increased performance and retention among new employees.[12] Two prominent findings were related to performance and attrition, revealing that "highly committed employees try 57 percent harder, perform 20 percent better, and are 87 percent less likely to leave than employees with low levels of commitment."[13]

While effective onboarding can last for more than a year, two significant benchmarks for new employees are the first week and the first ninety days.[14] After surveying new employees at Microsoft after their first week on the job and again after ninety days, researchers found that "little things matter most to hires—like having a working computer and immediate access to the building, email, and the intranet on day one"[15] They also determined that new employees who met with their manager during their first week on the job presented early growth in the following areas:[16]

1. These employees "tended to have a 12% larger internal network and double network centrality within 90 days." Better social connections for new employees provide a sense of belonging and more of a long-term investment in the organization.
2. They had "higher-quality meetings," which involve fewer people, are less than one hour and attendees are more engaged.
3. Increased collaboration in which "they spent nearly three times as much time collaborating with their team as those who did not have a one-on-one meeting."

Clearly, the manner in which new hires are brought into any organization is important and can benefit both the employee in terms of increased job productivity and longevity as well as the organization through retaining a quality hire and saving indirect costs associated with turnover. In addition, an organization full of engaged, satisfied, and productive people creates a culture that will attract other, like-minded individuals.

ONBOARDING PROCESS

What does effective onboarding look like? Onboarding approaches vary among organizations, consisting of informal and formal practices. Informal onboarding is ineffective and lacks structure as employees are left to learn on the job in a "sink or swim" mentality.[17] Formal onboarding, however, is designed to "assist an employee in adjusting to his or her new job in terms of both tasks and socialization," and consists of four levels: Compliance, Clarification, Culture, and Connection.[18]

Compliance

Compliance is the lowest onboarding level and involves employees learning about essential expectations such as how to submit sick leave, dress codes, and being mindful of any legal issues such as the Family Education Rights and Privacy Act (FERPA), which is important in higher education. Overall, compliance teaches new hires what they need to minimally function and survive on a daily basis.

Clarification

The next level of onboarding, clarification, teaches new hires about the expectations of their job, such as becoming familiar with promotion and tenure guidelines, required office hours and procedures for funding requests. Additionally, this level ensures new employees understand the organizational chart, such as their immediate supervisor, and are familiar with the entire organization. For example, in a university, this would include teaching new hires about the reporting structure within both student and academic affairs.

Culture

As the name implies, the culture level of onboarding gives new hires a sense of the cultural norms and values of the organization, which can often be hidden or unwritten. Nonetheless, this is a critical stage because it represents the uniqueness of the organization, providing a sense of belonging. In a university department, this stage might involve formal and informal mentoring sessions in which new hires learn about the history and values of the department and university. For example, this may include learning about the quality of leadership on campus or the overall work ethic.

Connection

Connection is the highest level of onboarding and consists of the relationships and networks that new employees will form throughout the organization, solidifying their sense of belonging and ownership. For example, it's important for new hires to not only form relationships within their academic departments but to also build networks across campus, building personal and professional equity.

ACADEMIC DEPARTMENT ONBOARDING

Onboarding a new hire within your department oftentimes begins during the first interactions you have with the individual during the interview process. By the time they accept the offer, you should have already established a working relationship with them. Every interaction matters and sends messages that are either in support of or against the department's culture and values. Remember, you may be the first and only lifeline for a new hire until they get settled into their new office and become acclimated to the community, especially if they're moving across the country to take the job. Therefore, make yourself available in case they need anything, job related or otherwise.

In addition, most universities have some type of new employee orientation that can vary from an online training seminar to one or more days on campus. While these are important and worthwhile experiences, they should serve to complement and not replace the onboarding experience from within the academic department. The department's administrative assistant can and should play a key role in the onboarding of all new hires as they will be responsible for a significant number of "getting started" items. Although not an extensive list, the following are examples of onboarding tasks ranging from administrative to cultural acclimation.

- Determine the location of the new hire's office and order common supplies.
- Order or create a name tag, office signs, and business cards ensuring the correct title, spelling, and title designation, such as "Dr."
- Determine the technology preferences (computer, programs, screens, etc.) and order them in a timely manner.
- Make necessary updates to the campus course schedule to reflect the new hire.
- Create a swag bag that has items related to the department and/or university, such as pens, notepads, a water bottle, or coffee cup.
- Check with your local chamber of commerce to see if they could also provide materials, including gift certificates to local businesses.

- Identify at least one person within the department who would be willing to serve as the "go-to" person for the new hire, providing information and, hopefully, mentoring.
- If possible, try to determine if there are other faculty members on campus who may share commonalities with the new hire, such as having degrees from the same institution and try to introduce them.
- Develop a plan for how you see the new hire contributing to the department, including committee appointments and share that with them during your first-week meeting.
- Make it a point to follow up with the new hire a few days before the semester officially starts to see how they're doing and if they need anything.
- Always make it a point to introduce the new hire to others when you are with them, especially members of upper administration, such as the Dean and Provost. Never pass up a chance to help the new hire network on and off-campus.
- If your university has special functions on campus or within the community for new hires and you're invited, you should go to support your new hire and also introduce them to others.

This is a very brief list that may seem procedural but will also help promote and establish the culture of the department while providing the new hire with the appropriate connections. Because of this, do not underestimate the importance of the location of the new hire's office. If possible, think about one or two mentors within the department that would be a good fit and try to place them in proximity of each other. Furthermore, depending upon the size and style of the main department and location of faculty offices, try to ensure that the new hire's office is close to others in the department and not in another part of the building. From the first day they come on campus, new colleagues should feel welcomed and have the chance to observe and interact with the day-to-day functions and conversations that take place in the department.

As noted in the previous list, schedule two important meetings with the new hire for the first week of the semester and ninety days later. These will obviously not be the only times you interact or even have a formal meeting with this person, but it's crucial to meet at one-week and ninety days. In the first meeting, ask them if they have everything they need to be successful and if not, what you can do for them.

Additionally, get their initial impressions of the department, college, and university since new perspectives are often the most accurate. Also take time to share your vision for how they will be a great addition to the department, focusing on their strengths and areas in which they can continue to grow. In fact, share with them the reasons they were hired, noting that hiring is one of the most important things you do and you always go after the best people.

Finally, ask them for their short- and long-term goals and how you can support those as their chair.

The conversation and questions during the ninety-day meeting may be similar in terms of asking the new hire if they have everything they need and what you can do to support them. In addition, asking them to share their positive and negative perceptions of their job, colleagues, department, university, and so on is very valuable information as it sheds light on the current culture that exists within the department. Even if it seems as though things are going well, there's always room for improvement and the views of a committed, yet relatively new outsider can be invaluable.

OFFBOARDING

Even though new hires are brought into the department with the hope of longevity and prosperity, there's a good chance that, as the chair, you will also have people leave for a variety of reasons, which may or may not have to do with you, the department or university. Regardless of the circumstances, there are a few guidelines to consider because how someone leaves an organization is just as important as how they came in.

Similar to onboarding, "offboarding" refers to "the separation process when an employee leaves a company."[19] Although there are standard procedures that must be accomplished such as turning in their keys and computer and finalizing paperwork with Human Resources, take the time to schedule a meeting with the outgoing faculty member. Please note that, depending upon the policies of the university, this may also be considered an official "exit interview" so be sure to comply with protocol, such as providing proper documentation.

Regardless of how the meeting is viewed by the university, it should have two main objectives: (1) to bring closure to the professional relationship and (2) to serve as an opportunity to hear their honest opinions of the department and suggestions for improvement. (Yes, this might be a bit uncomfortable depending upon why they are leaving but it's still beneficial.)

In the end, character always comes out on the way out.

Even with the best hiring committees and onboarding processes, when someone is entering an organization, they show their credentials; when they leave, they show their character. Therefore, in addition to thanking the outgoing faculty member for their service and contributions, also impress upon them the importance of showing good character on the way out. Once someone knows they're leaving the department and university, it could be tempting to say and do things that are unprofessional. Even if they have legitimate reasons to be disgruntled, the way people leave an organization is oftentimes how they're remembered. As Warren Buffet said, "It takes 20 years to build a reputation and five minutes to ruin it."[20] In the end, character always comes out on the way out so help outgoing faculty members realize the significance and long-term effects of the character they display as they leave the department and the university.

Finally, use the final meeting with the outgoing faculty member to get their honest opinions of the strengths, weaknesses, and areas in need of improvement within the department. Ironically, the best faculty members are oftentimes too professional to share their honest opinions with the chair. However, their opinions and perspective are usually very valid and insightful. Therefore, give them permission to tell you what you need to hear related to how the department could improve. This also includes having the courage to ask them how you could improve as a leader. In the end, wish them well and let them know they can always contact you if they need anything.

From the first time a candidate interacts with the search committee to their final meeting prior to leaving the university, onboarding and offboarding require persistent and effective leadership. Hiring great people who are talented enough to work elsewhere but, for a given length of time, choose to work in your department makes everyone better, causing "all boats to rise." Granted, it can be difficult to see great people move on, but if they leave on positive terms and show good character on the way out, then both you and your department are better for having worked with them. In the end, hiring great people takes great effort, but is always worth it.

Chapter 14

Student Leadership

They ask me why I teach and I reply, "Where could I find more splendid company?"

—Glennice L. Harmon

The two things that must be present for any type of educational institution to exist are students and teachers. As a department chair, you have an awesome opportunity and responsibility to serve both of these invaluable groups of people. While the previous chapters have focused on effectively leading the faculty and staff in your department, it's important to realize that you are also responsible for the students. Therefore, the purpose of this chapter is to provide an overview of effective principles for student-based leadership, which includes reviewing your leadership mission statement, being visible to students and advocating for them and how to address student-related conflict.

Even though the demands of the chair position may require you to give up some, if not all, of your teaching responsibilities, you can nonetheless continue to have a significant impact on your students. In many ways, one of the benefits of the elevated perspective of the chair position is that your actions and decisions can affect more students than you could have as a professor. In fact, as the chair, you should be one of the biggest advocates for the students in your department by supporting their instructors and overseeing quality programs that support student success. The tenets of effective leadership are somewhat universal; leading students is similar to leading your faculty members. Therefore, effective student leadership involves the following:

- Review your mission statement
- Be visible
- Be an advocate
- Address student conflict

REVIEW YOUR MISSION STATEMENT

While the principles of effective leadership can be applicable across multiple scenarios, it's important to revisit your leadership mission statement to determine if it's relevant to leading students. To begin, answer the following questions:

1. How do you define educational leadership in terms of supporting students' academic success?
2. To what extent are you comfortable providing academic leadership to your department? This may include performing in-class instructional evaluations along with leading curriculum and assessment initiatives.
3. Are you comfortable working with and presenting to students in large/small and formal/informal settings?
4. Do you have experience addressing student-related conflict?
5. When it comes to conflict, do you have a preference between having an uncomfortable conversation with a student or a faculty? Do you feel the same about both?
6. Do you have "teaching mentors" whom you can consult to assist you with student and academic leadership in higher education?
7. How are students motivated? Why do students choose to misbehave or make poor choices?
8. How comfortable are you interacting and developing relationships with both undergraduate and graduate students?
9. Think back to your time as a college student and try to identify people who impacted your life, both personally and academically. What did they do and how did they make you feel?
10. When thinking about your role as the academic leader of your department and its impact on students, what is your biggest concern or area in need of improvement?

Next, identify the key verbs and adjectives in your answers and consider sharing them with a trusted friend or colleague. Do your responses reflect a student-centered mindset? Are you confident and eager to serve the students in your department? Review the mission statement you developed as part of your leadership philosophy in chapter 1. To what extent does it accommodate student success through academic and nonacademic programming?

BE VISIBLE

Even though your chair duties may take you away from the classroom and other student-based activities, as the leader of the department, you are still responsible for the academic experience of each and every student. In addition, being the full-time billboard for your department involves professionally and ethically representing faculty members and students alike. It takes a village to raise a student through an academic program and you're in charge of that village.

Therefore, just like you make it a point to interact with your faculty (i.e., do your daily rounds), ensure that your students regularly see and interact with you. For example, try to attend some of the departmental and campus activities in which your students participate. While the relationships you build with them won't be the same as with your faculty, you can still make a connection and perhaps a lasting impact. In fact, your interactions with students contribute to the academic culture in which they reside, thus affecting their short- and long-term success.

In addition to being visible to your current students, it's also important to interact with potential students, which underscores the importance of overseeing an effective recruiting plan for all students (undergraduate and graduate) within all modalities (on-campus and virtual). For example, make sure your department has a positive and proactive marketing and social media presence, focusing on student opportunities and successes. Also use these venues to promote your faculty's accomplishments and how they support students.

Finally, develop a structured protocol for how members of your department meet and interact with prospective students during campus visits. Be intentional about whom they meet, how they are treated, and ensure some type of follow-up, be it a short email, phone call, or a handwritten note.

BE AN ADVOCATE

Although you can't teach every student in your department, as the chair, you can still influence their academic experiences and subsequent success through overseeing and supporting effective initiatives. In 2008, George Kuh's report titled *High-Impact Educational Practices: What They Are, Who Has Access to Them, and Why They Matter*[1] offered a framework of ten teaching and learning practices that "positively reinforce students' engagement, deep learning, gains in personal development outcomes, and retention."[2] While it's common to combine some of the high-impact practices within programs, the following provides a brief overview of each of the practices.[3]

1. First-Year Seminars and Experiences
   - Designed to bring small groups of students and faculty together in order to collaborate, with an emphasis on developing students' intellectual and practical competencies.

2. Common Intellectual Experiences
   • Includes a set of common, required classes, such as a general educa-
     tion program or experiences based upon a common major, minor, or
     other area of emphasis.
3. Learning Communities:
   • Designed to "encourage the integration of learning across courses
     and to involve students with 'big questions' that matter beyond the
     classroom."[4]
4. Writing-Intensive Courses
   • Courses designed to infuse writing across the college curriculum
     which are most effective when coordinated across the entire univer-
     sity to ensure depth and breadth of writing functions and genres.
5. Collaborative Assignments and Projects
   • Designed to enable students to collaboratively learn and solve problems,
     especially alongside those with diverse backgrounds and experiences.
6. Undergraduate Research
   • Designed to actively engage students across all disciplines in the
     research process both within and outside of the classroom.
7. Diversity/Global Learning
   • Enables students to "explore cultures, life experiences, and world-
     views different from their own"[5] and can include intercultural studies
     and experiential learning such as study abroad.
8. Service Learning, Community-Based Learning
   • Focuses on providing students real-life experiences within their com-
     munities that relate to areas they are studying across the curriculum.
9. Internships
   • Similar to service and community-based learning, internships provide
     students direct, hands-on experience related to their major programs
     and/or future careers. In addition, this frequently involves a supervi-
     sor within the field from whom students can learn.
10. Capstone Courses and Projects
    • Housed within a course or as a stand-alone degree requirement, these
      summative assessments represent a culminating experience in which
      students produce a product that reflects the essential objectives of
      their programs of study.

As the leader of your department, one way to advocate for undergraduate
students' academic development and overall experience in your program is to
consider adopting one or more of the aforementioned high-impact practices.
Students who participate in these activities have "significantly higher perceived development in leadership and multicultural competence."[6] Therefore,
while it's likely that your university is aware of and already implementing

these practices in other areas, work with your faculty (i.e., know your roster) to identify areas in which you could adopt and incorporate one or more of these high-impact practices.

For example, a logical first step is to consider an undergraduate research program in which interested faculty members work with students to conduct discipline-related scholarship or creative activity. Begin by assessing the level of interest among your faculty members and, if possible, offer financial support which could include funds for the student and faculty member to co-present at a national conference. Also consider a department-sponsored event in which students and faculty can share their work with the public.

In addition to implementing an undergraduate research program within your department, consider working with your colleagues in student affairs or admissions to establish a learning community. While this takes more planning and support than undergraduate research, it can be used to house other high-impact practices. The overall goal of the learning community is to provide students who are interested in a common theme, subject or major (as represented by your department) to form a small community that offers personal and academic support, similar to a family.

Although the details will vary based upon the structure and support of each campus, ideally, students in learning communities are identified prior to coming to campus as freshmen and are able to live in a shared, dedicated space, such as a dormitory. In addition, these students take many of the same classes, oftentimes being required to take at least one class as an entire group each semester, which is an example of a common intellectual experience. The students in this community could also be required to take a student success or freshmen seminar, thus incorporating another high-impact practice. Finally, students in a learning community should also have structured social experiences outside of the classroom in which to further develop relationships and form a sense of community.

Additional high-impact practices that can be incorporated into a learning community include service-based learning, internships, collaborative assessments and projects, and diversity/global learning, which includes study abroad. Furthermore, learning communities tend to focus on first-time, on-campus students, which can be an effective way to introduce students to the benefits of the academic programs within your department and, most importantly, enable them to build relationships with your faculty.

In addition to implementing high-impact practices, also consider sponsoring or adopting state- and national-level student organizations related to your department's academic area and/or related professional industries. Students who take part in these experiences are not only more engaged in your department but can begin to develop professional skills, which includes networking for future career opportunities.

Finally, related to student engagement within your department, follow the appropriate protocol, which may include consulting with your Dean, to establish a relationship with your foundation in order to develop department-specific student scholarships. It's likely that your department will already have specific scholarships, which can be a logical place upon which to build future financial support for your students.

Even though it may seem like you have fewer opportunities to interact with students than you did as a full-time faculty member, as the chair of your department, you have the opportunity and authority to significantly impact them—professionally and personally—through advocacy and oversight of quality programs and experiences.

ADDRESS STUDENT CONFLICT

As discussed in a previous chapter, being a leader means you're in the people business, which means courageously confronting conflict. Even though the majority of the conflict you address will involve your faculty and staff, it's important to realize that, as the leader of the department, you must also address student issues. As a faculty member, you most likely experienced student-related conflict in areas such as teaching, advising, and supervising projects. You will continue to address some of these same conflicts, along with those you didn't encounter as a faculty member. However, remember that as the leader of your department your actions are magnified and can significantly impact students.

While the information presented in previous chapters related to conflict are certainly applicable to and effective with students, the following illuminates some of the unique aspects of student-related conflict.

Please note that while you will be able to resolve most student-related conflict at your level, there will be times that you have a legal obligation to notify the proper authorities both on and off of your campus so always follow the appropriate reporting protocol.

Remember to LOVE

As a gentle reminder, remember that "people" means everyone, including students. Therefore, similar to your own faculty and staff, lead students with love, which means you still might not be happy with them or even approve of their behavior but can lovingly be firm and hold them accountable. In addition, always be honest and willing to admit your mistakes, which means offering a sincere apology when required. Remember to LOVE the students (i.e. others) you serve:

- **L**ead
- **O**thers with
- **V**ulnerability and
- **E**mpathy

In addition, remember that students, regardless of their age and life circumstances, are not only the most important group of people a university serves but they are choosing to attend your university and study in your department to learn and presumably enhance their overall life trajectory. Therefore, remember that every encounter you have with a student should be a learning experience in which your primary goal is to help them improve.

Support Your Faculty

Oftentimes, the student-related conflict you address will involve an argument or disagreement with a faculty member, usually related to a class grade or some other interpretation of a class policy. While there are times that, unfortunately, faculty members are at fault, it is also quite common for students to somewhat hastily assume they have been mistreated and/or to embellish or simply make up false accusations. In fact, your first question should always be "Have you visited with your professor about this?" often followed with "What does the syllabus say?"

In addition, be mindful of the duality of your role as chair when trying to resolve conflict between students and faculty. You need to be respectful of students' concerns but also handle the situation in such a way that enables you to honor the faculty members' reputation. Therefore, always ask the student the manner in which they would like you to share their concern with the faculty member, which usually results in one of the following options:

1. Share the student's name and concern immediately
2. Share the student's concern, but not their name, immediately
3. Share the student's name and concern after the class has ended
4. Share the student's concern, but not their name, after the class had ended
5. The student doesn't want you to share their name or concern—they just want you to be aware of the issue

Above all, always support your faculty by assuming they followed protocol and the student's complaint is perhaps an honest misunderstanding. Never speak negatively about one of your faculty members to another student, regardless of who is at fault. Doing so is not only unprofessional but may form a negative and permanent nexus or connection between the student's perception of that professor and their ability to provide an effective and unbiased educational experience.

STUDENT CONFLICT CONSIDERATIONS

The following will provide three separate scenarios and related dialogues for addressing common instances of student-related conflict. As presented in chapter 8, always consider the following, pre-conflict checklist, which has been updated for working with students.

1. Seven, nine, crime, or dime?
   - Always make sure that a crime didn't occur and that the student's rights were not violated, which includes policies specific to the university.
   - A student-specific addendum to this is in instances that involve student–student or student–faculty conflict, always determine if any type of inappropriate language or physical touch occurred, which needs to be reported immediately.
2. Why do you lead?
   - Revisit your mission statement, focusing on its relevance to and inclusion of students.
3. Whom do you serve?
   - As the leader of your department, you show up each day to serve all stakeholders, including students, faculty, and staff.
4. Have you built relationships?
   - While not at the level of relationships built with your faculty, still consider the extent to which you know the particular student and/or if they know you.
5. Do your homework.
   - Take the time to collect all of the facts and relevant documents. This may include but is not limited to viewing the student's file, visiting with the student's professor and reviewing the course syllabus.
6. Transpose the problem.
   - Think of the student who would be least likely to be in the situation and consider how you would respond to them. The student with whom you are interacting deserves the same consideration.
7. Reflect your culture.
   - Think about the type of culture and associated expectations you and your faculty have for your students and behave accordingly.

8. Choose courage.
   - Conflict can be uncomfortable so remember you're in the people business and the message you send to one student is what you send to every student. Do your job and choose courage.
9. Rationalize your fear
   - Conflict can cause fear, most of which is not rationale. However, reflect upon the previous steps, keeping in mind you are there to serve and educate all students, including the one with whom you will have the conflict conversation.

In addition, be mindful of the power differential that exists between you and the students. As the chair, you hold a significant amount of inherent power; you're an authority figure on campus. Furthermore, while students certainly have rights and are protected within the university system, unlike faculty members, they are not employees, they don't have tenure and they are not represented by a union. Therefore, always approach student conflict with a heightened sense of awareness, keeping in mind that your encounter should be a learning/growth experience for the student. Finally, always err on the side of caution and notify your Dean of the conflict scenario, along with a follow up of the conversation to ensure you are following protocol and honoring the rights of all involved parties.

The remainder of this chapter will present four conflict scenarios involving students. While the topics are somewhat common, the names and scenarios are completely fictional and intended to be a practical demonstration of the concepts associated with effectively managing student-related conflict.

STUDENT CONFLICT SCENARIO A

Dr. A has informed you that she suspects one of her students has plagiarized an assignment by taking it directly from another student (from a previous semester), only modifying the student's name and date. When Dr. A confronted the student, he claimed it was an honest mistake. He had been using his friend's materials to study but accidentally uploaded the wrong assignment to the course management system. Dr. A informs you that the student has been very dedicated throughout the semester and, as an instructor, she feels a bit uncomfortable confronting them, especially since they have denied the allegation. As the chair, you contact the student and set up a meeting in your office. Dr. A has requested that she not be there since it's the middle of the semester and she fears retaliation in the form of scathing teaching evaluations.

Chair: Good morning! Thank you for agreeing to meet with me on such short notice. Please take a seat.

Student: OK. You said in your email that Dr. A thinks I cheated off of a friend but that's not true.

Chair: Here's where we're at. I have visited with Dr. A and have reviewed the document. I have also asked our IT department on campus to dig into the document a bit deeper and it's clear that you submitted someone else's work. I can show you when the document was created and by whom.

Student: Well, yeah. That's what I told Dr. A My friend took her class last year and gave me the notes and assignments to study and I accidentally uploaded the wrong document.

Chair: OK. I understand this happened two days ago. Did Dr. A tell you to submit the actual assignment, the one you did, so you could receive credit?

Student: She asked for it but I couldn't find it. Honestly, I've had computer problems all semester so I asked her if I could have a few extra days to re-do the assignment but she said "no" and gave me an "F."

Chair: So, you've had computer problems all semester?

Student: Yes. It's happened in all my classes.

Chair: Really? How many other classes have you failed to turn in assignments because of computer problems? I ask because it looks like your mid-term grades were all "B's or "A's."

Student: Well, actually, it was just this class. My computer isn't great but I'm usually able to get it to work.

Chair: Please be honest. Did you knowingly submit someone else's work as your own?

Student: I submitted my friend's paper but it was a mistake.

Chair: Here's the deal. I understand mistakes happen but your name was on the document along with the due date, which tells me you knowingly updated and submitted someone else's work. Is this what happened?

Student: Yeah. I've been busy and I have a good grade in that class and, besides, everyone cheats in there so it's not just me.

Chair: I appreciate you sharing that information but we're here to talk about you. As noted in the syllabus, Dr. A could fail you for the entire course due to one instance of plagiarism. Are you aware of that?

Student: I am now. So, am I going to fail the class?

Chair: Luckily, Dr. A tells me you're a good student with a lot of potential. You simply made a bad choice. So, Dr. A and I have decided your grade of "F" will remain but you still can come out of the class with decent grade as long as this is the last time we have this conversation. Do you understand the decision and expectations moving forward?

Student: Yes, I understand. I'm sorry—it won't happen again.

Chair: I believe you. Overall, we just want you to be successful in our program so you have to make good choices. One last thing, I'm going to write up a brief description of our conversation today, which will include that you understand you will fail that assignment and what the consequences will be if it happens again. Could you reply to my email to indicate you received it and understand?

Student: Yes. I can do that.

Chair: Alright. That's about it. I realize this was a bit uncomfortable but as far as I'm concerned, it's in the past. I look forward to us having great, positive conversations in the future. Please let me know if you have questions and if I can ever help you out in any way. OK?

Student: Thank you. I appreciate it.

STUDENT CONFLICT SCENARIO B

You have received an email from Jordan, an upper-level student in your program whom you know as they are very active in your department as well as on campus. In their email, Jordan shares that they would like to meet with you to share concerns about Dr. B's in-class behavior, which they describe as unprofessional. In addition, Jordan indicates that this is a shared concern and, as a result, Jordan has been asked to also represent the views and concerns of four other students in the class. You reply to Jordan's email, thanking them for sharing the concern and indicate you would like to meet with them the following morning.

Chair: Good morning, Jordan! Have a seat. Thanks for coming in on short notice. It's nice to see you again.

Jordan: Thanks, Dr. Chair. I appreciate your quick reply. I hope you don't think I'm trying to get Dr. B in trouble. I kind of feel bad sending you that email.

Chair: No worries. My door is always open to students. Before we get much further, I do have an important question. You describe Dr. B's behavior as unprofessional. At any time has he used inappropriate language, such as swearing or derogatory terms or engaged in any type unwelcome physical interactions with students?

Jordan: Um, no. Not really. No. He hasn't. Sorry, I had to think.

Chair: Thank you. I realize that might be an odd question but I have to ask. Also, I want you to know that I have not yet brought this to Dr. B's attention since I wanted to meet with you first. However, I may have to share this with him but will do so in a way you're comfortable with. So, please tell me your concerns. I'm going to be taking notes but please know I'm paying attention to you.

Jordan: That's fine. Well, Dr. B is very smart and knows what he's talking about. Some of the students really like him. But, it's like he tries too hard to get all the students to like him and seem popular and cool.

Chair: Can you be more specific about what he does to get students to like him and seem popular? What have you heard and observed?

Jordan: Well, the main thing is he always tries to make jokes about getting drunk and going to parties and assumes that we're all wild, hard-drinking college students.

Chair: OK. Can you provide specific examples of comments he has made?

Jordan: Well, a few weeks ago on a Friday, he reminded us that we had a test coming up on Monday so to make sure we studied before we went out and got drunk because it's hard to study with a hangover. Another time, he was trying to get us to talk more in a class discussion because it was pretty quiet so he asked if he should have made it into a drinking game to get people involved.

Chair: Alright. Anything else you think I should know? Your email mentioned you were somewhat representing other students with this concern.

Jordan: There's just a group of us that kinda hang out outside of class and it just bothers us. I mean, Dr. B is a nice guy and I'm not trying to get him fired or anything. I just think he needs to know that it's just weird and uncomfortable when he makes those comments. It's always about drinking or being stereotypical colleges who just like to party. We just want to go to class to learn.

Chair: I completely understand, Jordan. We still have a few weeks left in the semester, what would you like to see happen here?

Jordan: Again, I don't want him to get in trouble. When he's not trying to be cool he's actually a pretty good professor. We're just tired of the comments. It's immature and gets old in a hurry.

Chair: OK. Please know that I am going to visit with Dr. B about this but want you to feel comfortable. At this point, I don't see a need to share your name unless you want me to. Also, I think he needs to know immediately—this can't wait until the end of the semester. What are you comfortable with?

Jordan: Um, I don't think he would be mad at me but I would prefer that you don't use my name if that's OK?

Chair: That's perfectly fine. Anything else you want to share? I just want to make sure you and your friends are comfortable in that class and get the experience you deserve.

Jordan: Yeah, it's fine. I mean, I'm not sure if I'll go out of my way to take another class with him but I think he just needs to know he shouldn't say those things.

Chair: If you think of anything else, please let me know. Thanks again for taking the initiative to visit with me. My door is always open so let me know if there's anything else. Have a nice day.

Jordan: Thanks. You, too—have a nice day.

STUDENT CONFLICT SCENARIO C

You receive an email from Dr. Z, who suggests you may want to visit with Taylor, a student in your department whom Dr. Z mentors in your undergraduate research program. Dr. Z suggests that there might be an issue between Taylor and Dr. C, a professor in your department who has Taylor is one of his seminar classes. Given your schedule, you have your administrative assistant call Taylor, asking if she could come visit with you later that afternoon, which she is able to do.

Chair: Hi, Taylor. I'm Dr. Chair. Have a seat. I don't believe we've met but Dr. Z tells me you're working on a great project together so I look forward to seeing it. Thanks for coming on short notice, I don't want to keep you too long. I understand there might be some issues between you and Dr. C?

Taylor: Thank you! Yeah, Dr. Z is great. But, yes, I didn't know where to start so I told Dr. Z I was concerned about Dr. C. She asked what was going on and I said he was being inappropriate in class so she suggested I talk to you since you're the chair.

Chair: OK. I'm glad to help. So, I assume you're in Dr. C's class?

Taylor: Yes. I'm in his morning seminar class.

Chair: OK. First of all, I know we just met so please know everything we discuss will be confidential but there might be things I have to share with other people above my head. So, this might seem a bit odd but I have to ask if, at any time, Dr. C has used inappropriate language, such as swearing or derogatory terms or engaged in any type of unwelcome physical interactions with you or other students in the class?

Taylor: Um, I'm not sure. I don't think so.

Chair: Again, this is confidential so if you can, please just tell me what's occurred and we'll go from there. I'm paying attention—I just need to take some notes, OK?

Taylor: Well, I feel bad and don't want to jeopardize my grade or get in trouble but during the second or third class of the semester, Dr. C stopped me after class and asked what I usually do on the weekends. He said I seemed pretty smart so he guessed I didn't have to study much. It was a bit weird but I thought he was just trying to get to know the students so I told him I usually work on the weekends.

Chair: OK. At that time did he touch you or do anything else that made you feel uncomfortable? Did he use other language that was inappropriate?

Taylor: No. That was it. But, the next week, he stopped me again after class and said he thought he saw me out at a restaurant the night before eating alone. He said he assumed someone like me would have a boyfriend so why wasn't he with me? I told him I wasn't out at any restaurants and ignored the boyfriend comment.

Chair: And when, exactly, did this conversation take place? Where was it?

Taylor: About 3 weeks ago on Tuesday morning after class.

Chair: Were you two in the classroom?

Taylor: Yes.

Chair: Was anyone else in there? Did anyone hear or see this?

Taylor: No, most people left quickly so it was just us.

Chair: Did he say anything else? Has he done or said anything since then?

Taylor: No, not really.

Chair: Not really?

Taylor: Well, he kinda smiles and winks at me in class sometimes but that's about it. A few times, he's patted me on the side of the shoulder telling me "good job" when we're discussing things in groups and he's walking around the room.

Chair: Have you shared these details and concerns with anyone else?

Taylor: No. I felt like I was being a bit dramatic and didn't want to get in trouble. It's been on my mind so I started to tell Dr. Z but just said there was an issue between us in class.

Chair: Taylor, I'm really sorry this happened and, to be honest, I need to do what's best for you and contact my Dean as well as our Compliance Department. I can't say for certain what will happen but I can tell you that I'm glad you shared this, you don't need to fear any type of consequences—from Dr. C or anyone—and we're going to do what we need to help you out. I would like to call our Compliance Officer right now and have you share what you just told me. Is that OK?

Taylor: Um, yeah. I can do that. This seems serious and scary. I hope I didn't get anyone in trouble.

Chair: You're fine. I really appreciate you sharing this with me. I'm going to make the call now and we'll go from there.

STUDENT CONFLICT SCENARIO D

Dr. D brings it to your attention that Taylor, a student in her class upper-level capstone class, is becoming increasingly rude to her and other students, oftentimes trying to control the discussion. In addition, when Dr. D and other students have politely tried to suggest that Taylor be respectful of others, he becomes more irritable. Recently, Taylor snapped back at another student, suggesting they lacked the intelligence to tell him what to do. Overall, despite his less-than-professional behavior in class, Taylor is very academically capable and will most likely finish the term with a high grade. Dr. D has asked you to visit with Taylor in an attempt to rectify his behavior. After sending him an email providing a brief overview of the purpose of the meeting, he agrees to meet you the following afternoon in your office.

Chair: Good afternoon, Taylor. Thanks for stopping by. Please have a seat. Can I get you anything?

Taylor: No. I'm fine. I really can't stay long so can you just tell me what this is all about?

Chair: Of course. As I shared in the email, Dr. D has indicated that while you are doing very well in her class in terms of academic performance and she certainly encourages all of her students to engage in active discussions, it seems as though you have been rather eager, some might say aggressive, in your overall tone and need to control the conversation. Is this accurate?

Taylor: Maybe. I don't know. I mean, it gets kinda boring because no one really understands much in there. I'm probably the smartest person in the class so I don't think I should have to listen to people who know less than I do.

Chair: OK. I also understand that earlier in the week you told another student they weren't smart enough to tell you what to do. Is this accurate?

Taylor: Yeah. I mean, I wasn't trying to be rude but come on, that person clearly doesn't know what's going on. They don't even come to class regularly. Don't try to tell me I don't know what I'm talking about when you can't even show up enough to form an opinion. You know?

Chair: So, Taylor, it seems like you value discipline and consistency?

Taylor: What do you mean?

Chair: You said it bothers your when people fail to come to class or take the time to study and learn the material. Is this correct?

Taylor: Yeah, that's right. It's not a hard class so how lazy and ignorant do you have to be to not show and learn something?

Chair: Well, Taylor, I suspect you and Dr. D are probably on the same page in terms of expecting people to study the material and come to class. In fact, I know she speaks highly of your abilities to comprehend the material. However, it seems like there's a disconnect between your academic performance and in-class behavior. Is this accurate?

Taylor: I guess. It's just frustrating when people try to talk and not have anything important to say or contribute to the class.

Chair: So, it seems like you value a good, in-class discussion?

Taylor: Yes, I do.

Chair: Believe it or not, Dr. D and the rest of students also value in-class discussions, which is why they've been a bit frustrated when you try to dominate the conversation and suggest they're not smart enough to contribute. What do you think?

Taylor: That's probably true.

Chair: Well, then, here's where we're at. I'm confident you enjoy the class and actually respect Dr. D and the other students but it seems like you might get a big eager and say things that don't reflect your true character. Am I correct?

Taylor: Yes, that's it. I can get pretty animated.

Chair: OK. Well, do you think you can try to not dominate the conversation as much and certainly, refrain from being rude to other students? That's unacceptable and I know you're better than that.

Taylor: Yeah, I know. I'm sorry. I'll do it.

Chair: Great. I think we've come to an understanding here. Please know that both Dr. D and I think highly of you and want you to be successful, academically and professionally. So, I'll let Dr. D know we worked this out and I fully intend to get a good report from her in the future. If this sounds fair and you don't have any more questions, you're free to go.

Taylor: OK. I'm fine. Thank you.

Chair: Thank you. Have a nice day.

Chapter 15

Mentoring and Moving On

Someone's sitting in the shade today because someone planted a tree a long time ago.

—Warren Buffet

Eventually, it will be time to move on from the chair position, with only one of every five chairs moving upward on the administrative track.[1] Regardless of if you leave the position to retire, go back to faculty, leave higher education for another career, or pursue a deanship, it's important to know that it's normal to move on because even the best chairs can stay too long. Therefore, the purpose of this chapter is to offer guidance on when to know if you should stay in the chair position and grow or eventually go and pursue other opportunities. This will include realizing the extent to which you not only led but mentored others, thus affecting your legacy as the department chair and potential effectiveness in future leadership positions.

In their book *Department Chair Leadership Skills*, Gmelch and Miskin report that chairs must make a concerted effort to remain engaged in the position or will risk feeling as though they have plateaued. To avoid becoming stagnant or plateauing as a chair, the authors suggest "re-treading" as opposed to "retreating."[2] For example, seek opportunities to serve within your academic discipline or related to higher education leadership through national organizations. In other words, focus on challenges and tasks within your department, university, and profession to which you can contribute as opposed to simply maintaining the status quo.

However, sooner or later, you will most likely move on from the chair position to either go on to pursue additional administrative/leadership positions in higher education or return to the faculty ranks. To aid in your decision, consider the following:

- Revisit your purpose
- Assess your courage, character, and relationships
- Acknowledge your patterns
- Assess your investments
- Consider your legacy

REVISIT YOUR PURPOSE

Chapter 1 encouraged you to focus on your professional mission and purpose and the extent to which that aligned with your leadership philosophy. There are some aspects of your passion and sense of purpose that, regardless of your profession, will remain the same. However, after gaining experience as a department chair and presumably growing into a more effective leader, it's possible that you will identify a newfound passion in continuing to lead and serve others at the next level, most likely as a Dean.

Likewise, despite being a successful chair, the experience may only solidify the fact that your true passion and purpose lies within serving as a faculty member, working with students and advancing your scholarly agenda. Either way, there's isn't a bad or wrong decision to make as long as you accepted the chair position for the right reasons and worked to selflessly serve and influence others with courage and integrity. Therefore, give yourself permission to reflect on your purpose and passion to determine the next step.

COURAGE, CHARACTER, AND RELATIONSHIPS

In addition to revisiting your purpose and the extent to which it may have changed, take time to reflect upon your decisions as the department chair, focusing on your courage, character, and relationships. Identify some of the more prominent initiatives and successes of the faculty and students and ask yourself if it occurred because of or in spite of your courage, the character you displayed and the relationships you built.

Courage

Courage is so important to a leader that this book dedicates an entire chapter to the topic. Honestly, if you are feeling run down and worn out as a department chair, there's a good chance it's because you were not as courageous as you could have been. While leading with courage takes energy, not doing so can be debilitating. Therefore, choosing each day to lead with courage, while still demanding, will leave you with a feeling of confidence, knowing you performed within the best of your abilities. Looking back, whether you loved or loathed being the chair, in large part, is a function of if you led courageously. The following questions can help you further assess your leadership courage:

- How much did you contribute to the life cycle of problems? Did you make things better or worse? Will the person who follows you be left with a field full of problems or potential?
- How do you feel about conflict? Did you become comfortable with the uncomfortable or do you long for the days when a major conflict consisted of a student arguing a grade or asking for an assignment extension?
- How much of the chair duties would you have done without any pay increase from being a faculty member?

Character

In addition to acknowledging your courage, search your conscience and you will most likely have a sound understanding of the type of character you displayed as the chair. Think about your most difficult decisions and conversations—what did you ultimately do when no one else was looking? No one is perfect and leadership provides a buffet full of bad choices and decisions from which to sample but in the end, you know what's right and wrong and whether or not you had to compromise your integrity.

Looking back on your decisions, can you hold your head high and walk without shame, guilt, or condemnation because you have been truthful and above reproach? Whatever you compromise will ultimately control you. Therefore, the decisions and behaviors that still haunt you are an indicator of how much you had to compromise your character and integrity as a leader.

> Whatever you compromise will ultimately control you.

Relationships

As an effective, courageous leader, it's impossible to please all the people all of the time; you're going to have a few enemies. However, how would you describe the depth and breadth of the relationships you formed with those whom you served as well as with related stakeholders? Did you form authentic, albeit professional, relationships in which you not only got to know others but, most importantly, were vulnerable enough to let them know you? When you made mistakes, even with the best of intentions, did you call yourself out, and have a humble conversation with those whom you offended, offering a sincere apology?

In addition, are there common variables in your life that have enhanced or damaged your personal and professional relationships with others? Remember, the common variable in all of your life's decisions and relationships is *you*. You were present and responsible for all of it. Accordingly, what role do you tend to play in your positive and negative relationships and did this same pattern emerge as a leader? What can you learn from this and, overall, does your "people pattern" suggest you're able to establish and maintain healthy relationships?

Ultimately, even if you did an admirable job and the majority of people would be happy if you continued to serve as their chair, when it comes to relationships, intuition doesn't lie. As noted in previous chapters, being a chair means people and relationships are your business. Therefore, take time to assess whether or not you truly enjoyed building and sustaining relationships with others and if you would like that to be a critical and enhanced component of your next position.

ACKNOWLEDGE YOUR PATTERNS

For better or for worse, leaders leave an undeniable pattern that defines them. Some department chairs are so effective that regardless of the circumstances they inherit, within a short time, it becomes clear they are positively influencing the organization because a pattern emerges. The culture and morale improve and the relationships become authentic. In addition, initiatives such as new programs, external funding and student enrollment increase. Finally, the true culture keepers emerge and take ownership of the department, thus initiating a cycle of great people attracting other great people to the organization.

Remember, a person's true character always comes out on the way out of the organization. The pattern left behind by a chair reveals the unique and undeniable characteristics of their leadership DNA, which are also accurate predictors of their future success.

Great leaders are like a trusted chain restaurant because you always know what you're going to get. Therefore, assess your leadership patterns and tendencies. If you were to go somewhere else, would people know within a short time that you were there because you are overseeing and initiating similar outcomes as in previous positions? If so, what patterns and subsequent results have come to define your leadership?

ASSESS YOUR INVESTMENTS

Another part of being an effective leader is assessing the effect you have on others through mentoring. A leader who fails to identify and mentor other leaders, in part, has failed to lead. As previously shared, Brené Brown defines a leader as "anyone who takes responsibility for finding the potential in people and processes, and who has the courage to develop that potential."[3] Have you invested into others, mentoring them to become great leaders? Have you taken the time to form relationships in order to find and develop potential in others that they may not see in themselves?

> A leader who fails to identify and mentor other leaders, in part, has failed to lead.

Bestselling author Anthony Tjan, after having interviewed close to 100 well-known and respected leaders within a variety of industries, found that "they do everything they can to imprint their 'goodness' onto others in ways that make others feel like fuller versions of themselves."[4] He goes on to share four important things these leader-mentors do:[5]

1. Put the relationship before the mentorship
2. Focus on character rather than competency
3. Shout loudly with your optimism and keep quiet with your cynicism
4. Use the 24 × 3 rule (Spend twenty-four seconds, twenty-four minutes, or twenty-four hours thinking about all of the reasons that a mentee's idea is good before criticizing it)
5. Be more loyal to your mentee than you are to your company

How would you characterize your relationship with those you have mentored? Have you worked to put the relationships first, focusing on them as a person? Have you been positive, with a bias for offering praise over criticism? Would you be willing to stand up and potentially jeopardize your job if it meant being loyal to your mentee for the right reasons?

It's undeniable that great leadership requires investing in other people to help them reach their maximum potential. In addition, true mentoring comes from a place of caring and compassion in which the mentor sincerely wants what's best for the mentee, even if it means surpassing the mentor. Therefore, as you consider whether or not you should continue into another leadership position, step back and honestly assess if you have selflessly mentored and developed other leaders.

Mentoring Mirror

Remember that you're in the people business and while the majority of those whom you serve will not move into formal leadership roles, to modify an old saying, it not only "takes one to know one" but as a leader, it also "takes one to grow one." Accordingly, part of serving and developing others is having the ability to see their potential before they see it in themselves.

According to Mark Sanborn, a bestselling author and leadership authority, "Great leaders help people have a larger vision of themselves. Leaders look for the potential in followers that followers often don't recognize in themselves."[6] If you serve long enough as a leader you will ultimately attract and produce those who reflect your true character. Effective leadership is a team sport, starting with an inner circle of people. Look at your inner circle and consider if you are investing in others to develop them as leaders

> If you serve long enough as a leader, you will ultimately attract and reproduce those who reflect your true character.

If you want a glimpse of your mentoring abilities, look into your "Mentoring Mirror" by answering the following questions about those with whom you associate. This will tell you if you have produced other leaders and will be yet another indicator of your effectiveness in future leadership positions:

- Are you comfortable not being the smartest person in the room? Do you purposefully attract and mentor those who possess strengths and talents you do not have?
- Are you comfortable with mentees who are more skilled than you are at communicating and forming relationships? Are you comfortable if they are better at owning the room as a speaker and interacting with people in public?

- Are you truly committed to helping your mentees become the best they can be or is your actual message "be the best you can be as long as it's not better than me"?
- Are your mentees honest and have integrity? Do they actively challenge you and, when necessary, call you out, or do they just go along to get along?
- Are you challenged to become a better person and leader as a result of spending time with your mentees? Is the relationship reciprocal so that you learn as much from them as they do from you?
- When you look at the career trajectory of those you've mentored, what have they gone on to become and accomplish?
- Are you genuinely happy for your mentees' success?
- Do you continue to have a strong relationship with your mentees?

In addition, it's highly unlikely that as a successful department chair you have made it this far without having your own mentors who have spoken into your life, challenging you to become the best version of yourself. Therefore, please take time to thank those who have helped you along the way, acknowledging you wouldn't be where you are today without their support and dedication.

Finally, continue to seek new mentors who will help you grow both personally and professionally. Always be vulnerable enough to continue to learn and improve because those whom you serve are worth it. As Kevin Lawrence says in his book *Your Oxygen Mask First: 17 Habits to Help High Achievers Survive & Thrive in Leadership & Life*, "Keep creating opportunities to be a novice learning from masters."[7]

CONSIDER YOUR LEGACY

If after thoroughly reflecting on the various aspects of your purpose and leadership effectiveness, you determine that the time has come to leave the chair position and move up the higher education administrative ladder, reflect upon your legacy. At first, it may seem self-serving and arrogant to consider your legacy as a department chair. However, legacy is defined as "a gift by will, especially of money or other personal property" or as "something transmitted by or received from an ancestor or predecessor or from the past."[8] Your legacy as a chair will be the gifts and values you leave behind which are the result of a job well done in the service of others.

Another way to define a leader's legacy is the extent to which their actions affect those they will never meet. What gifts did they transmit or leave behind that will benefit others? Similar to the foundation of a house, if a leader does the right things, the right way, with and for the right people, the things they build will stand the test of time, serving students, faculty, and staff for years to come. Likewise, ineffective leaders tend to use inadequate materials, building a façade instead of a foundation that will neither last nor benefit others, frequently crumbling shortly after they leave the organization.

Therefore, considering your legacy as a chair is not selfish. Instead, it enables you to step back, take a breath and hopefully smile as you think about what you and your colleagues were able to accomplish, proving that, collectively, the whole was greater than the sum of its parts. Reflect on the programs and initiatives that will benefit students, faculty, and staff whom you will never meet. This isn't arrogant because in all honesty, most people won't know you were the chair within a few semesters of your departure, which is fine. However, you can still take pride in knowing you were able to help people and did it the right way.

In the end, leaving a positive legacy as a department chair has nothing to do with your fame, fortune, or whether or not they'll erect a statue in your honor or name a building after you. Leaving a positive legacy and knowing you did a good job can be summed up by answering the following questions affirmatively:

1. Did you leave the position, the organization, and, most importantly, the people better than you found them?
2. If given the opportunity, would the majority of people you worked with gladly work with you again?
3. Will the result of your actions have a positive impact on those whom you will never meet?

THE NEXT STEP

As you consider accepting another leadership position, such as becoming a Dean, revisit some of the reasons and questions presented in chapter 1, which focused on moving from a faculty member into the chair position. While each leadership position in higher education has its own unique aspects, the following reasons for not pursuing a leadership position remain valid. Therefore, as you look at the next step, review the "Foolish Four" reasons for which people should not become leaders:

1. No one else wants the job
2. Power and control
3. The money
4. Entitlement

In addition to the aforementioned reasons, answer the following questions as you consider moving on from the chair position to accept another leadership role in higher education:

- Where do you want to spend your bad days?
- Whom will you follow?
- Who will lead and mentor you?

Where Do You Want to Spend Your Bad Days?

This may seem like an odd or absurd question but it's legitimate. If you have made it to the point of considering or having an offer to move from a chair to a Dean position, you have clearly been successful at each level of your career within higher education. You're an intelligent, successful person, capable of setting and attaining goals. Therefore, regardless of your vocation and location, you will create your own success and have more good days than bad.

However, leaders truly earn their money making the difficult decisions on difficult days. Therefore, consider the difficult times and decisions you have already experienced as chair and, as you consider the next position and all it entails, ask yourself if you would be happy having bad days there. It's easy to be happy and motivated when things are going well but where do you want to be when you are challenged, when times are tough and when you have to lean into conflict and have difficult conversations?

Whom Will You Follow?

In addition to addressing conflict and making tough decisions, a contributing factor to the depth and breadth of your "bad days" in the next position is being aware of the person whom you will follow. For example, if you accept a Dean position, you must consider the overall profile, accomplishments, and leadership style of your predecessor. This is a delicate balancing act because following an effective leader increases the odds that you will inherit a somewhat stable and healthy organization and culture; following a bad leader means you have a significant renovation ahead of you.

Leadership is never easy so whom you follow will simply dictate the type of challenges you will face. If you follow a great leader, you could very well be held to an unfair and unattainable standard. Without realizing it, people in the organization will simply want you to maintain the status quo by being someone you're not. If you follow a less-than-effective leader, the good news is that instead of needing a ladder to reach the bar of expectations, you may need a shovel to raise it. Nonetheless, the people will still have a vision of who they want you to be, which will most likely be the opposite of your predecessor.

Given the variability of leaders and the culture of their respective universities, there isn't a clear-cut rule of whom you should and should not follow since every position will have its own set of unique challenges. However, do your homework and have a sound understanding of your predecessor and assess the pros and cons accordingly.

Who Will Lead and Mentor You?

As you move up the higher education administrative ladder, officially crossing the line from a chair to a Dean, the quality of your new bosses and leadership team is important as it contributes to both your professional growth and stability. Therefore, take time to learn about the overall leadership structure, philosophy, and history of the university. Remember, great leaders attract other great leaders so the fact that you're on their radar is usually a good sign. Nonetheless, do your homework to seek and ask questions that will reveal the type of leaders and mentors with and for whom you will work, such as

- Can they articulate their leadership style and philosophy?
- How do they address conflict?
- To what extent do they believe it's a leader's job to mentor and develop other leaders?
- Who are their leadership mentors?
- What are they currently reading or studying related to leadership?
- In what areas are they naturally intuitive?
- What's one thing they do on a daily basis focused on developing themselves as a leader?
- If given fifteen minutes to prepare for their TED-style talk, what would it be and why?
- What does their leadership pedigree look like in terms of what their mentors and mentees have done and/or gone on to accomplish?

Overall, research and interview your potential bosses, leaders, and mentors as you would one of your own candidates. In the end, care enough about yourself as a leader to demand that those who lead you have the ability and experience to challenge, develop and mentor you.

Serving as a department chair can be one of the most rewarding leadership positions one can hold in higher education; however, everyone eventually moves on, staying in an administrative role, going back to faculty, or perhaps retiring. Regardless of your post-chair plans, reflect upon the time you spent serving others as the department chair and the extent to which you were able to do so with courage and integrity, based upon positive, personal relationships.

Conclusion

As we come to the end of this book, I sincerely hope that what I have shared, in some way, will be of value to you as a leader as well as those you serve. The department chair position is one of the more challenging leadership roles in higher education and perhaps among all leadership positions. As chairs, we epitomize what it means to *lead from the middle* on a daily basis. In addition, the location of "the middle" is fluid and can change based on the person, procedure, policy, or conflict we're addressing. Some days, it may seem like we're walking a tightrope without a safety net, and in addition to being asked to make it across from one point to another, we also have to change our shoes in the process.

Even though the demands of the chair position are significantly different from what was required to be a successful faculty member, many of us still have to meet expectations in the areas of teaching, service, and scholarship in addition to being responsible for the people, programs, and protocols within our department. Furthermore, if we're in the position for the right reasons, much of our time or daily schedule is not our own. In fact, on a daily basis, we're not the most important person on our agenda, which requires adopting a selfless, servant-based attitude.

As chairs, we're always communicating and sending messages, even when we say nothing at all. This extends beyond our office, the campus, and certainly outside of typical business hours. Part of walking the leadership tightrope means we're *always* the leader and human billboard for our department and everyone it represents. This is a nonnegotiable, inherent part of almost every leadership position. Even though it may not seem like it, none of us were actually forced to accept the chair position, moving beyond our tenure-track appointments; being a chair is not a promotion and tenure requirement.

To be honest, I would submit that serving in any type of leadership role is more than a choice; it's a calling.

Although it can be a bit daunting to think about the awesome responsibility that we must accept on a daily basis, for some people, the "deal breaker" is the realization that, as a leader, courage is not optional. We show up each and every day to face and address some form of conflict, which takes courage. In fact, how we address conflict (or failure to do so) is perhaps the most consistent and substantial message we send to those we serve. Remember, we encourage what we tolerate and normalize what we ignore. And if we ignore problems, they never really go away but simply grow exponentially day-by-day.

As Jeffrey Buller said, "The job of chairing a department is probably the most important, least appreciated, and toughest administrative position in higher education."[1] While I'm honored and humbled that you have made it to this point in the book, you may still be asking yourself why would anyone in their right mind want to be a department chair, especially since most people receive little to no training for the position. In addition, the training and skills required to be a successful faculty member will not, by themselves, prepare someone to effectively lead an academic department. So, why do we serve and lead as chairs?

In chapter 1, I encouraged you to develop your purpose or mission statement as leader, which should be applicable to your position as a department chair. I began my career as a public school teacher and will always consider myself, first and foremost, an educator who is dedicated to serving students. For example, in my current position, while I may not teach or directly interact with all of the students (i.e., future teachers) in our program, I still consider myself responsible for their education, especially since it will ultimately impact the lives of the students they will teach. Therefore, as the chair of a Department of Teacher Education, my mission is "To serve those who will serve others." This is further guided and informed by my definition of leadership, which is influence through character, courage, relationships, and service.

In addition to developing your mission statement for leading as a department chair, I now want you to dig a bit deeper and consider what Simon Sinek refers to as your "Just Cause," which is a "specific vision of a future state that does not yet exist; a future state so appealing that people are willing to make sacrifices in order to help advance toward that vision."[2] A true Just Cause has to benefit others and may be so audacious that you could spend a lifetime trying to contribute to or create a world in which it might someday exist.

To further illustrate the differences between a mission, or "why," and a Just Cause, Sinek says, "Think of the WHY like the foundation of a house, it is the starting point. It gives whatever we build upon it strength and permanence. Our Just Cause is the ideal vision of the house we hope to build."[3]

For example, I believe that it's possible to improve people's lives by improving their leaders. Because of this, my Just Cause is *to create and contribute to a world in which people are empowered to reach their potential and live better lives because they have better leaders.* While our mission statements can be modified as we mature and progress through our careers, it's possible to adopt or join a Just Cause that will remain constant. I feel fortunate that my mission and purpose for leading as a department chair also contributes to my Just Cause. In addition, I am hopeful that this book, in some way, will help train and develop effective leaders who will ultimately lead others in a way that empowers them to lead fulfilling lives.

Therefore, as we bring this journey to an end, I want to pose a few final thoughts, questions, and suggestions that will hopefully encourage you to continue to develop yourself as not only a great department chair but also as a life-long learner and leader.

Go back and reflect upon what you have learned as a result of reading this book. What areas related to your purpose and mission for leading have remained the same or perhaps been reinforced and in what areas have you been encouraged to grow? Make a list or "action plan" in which you identify what you will do on a daily basis to improve as a leader. In addition to revisiting your purpose and mission statement, what is your Just Cause and to what extent are you able to pursue and contribute to this while leading as a department chair?

Great leaders are great mentors. Who are you currently mentoring? In addition, try to identify another person to develop and mentor. This person doesn't necessarily have to be someone within your department or who reports to you. An effective mentoring relationship is more about connecting our purpose and passion as opposed to simply finding someone with a similar title or even within our own organization. Therefore, take someone with you. Replicate other great leaders who will go on and repeat the process. Remember, a true legacy can be defined as the extent to which we influence those whom we will never meet.

Even though the department chair is the epitome of "leading from the middle," please realize that no matter how far you advance as a leader, you will always be leading from the middle of something. By virtue of serving others, you will have to lead and represent those who report to you while also serving your superiors. In fact, one of the many benefits of serving as a chair is that it provides valuable experiences that will certainly make you a better leader if and when you move into other administrative positions.

People and relationships matter. As a leader, you're in the people business and regardless of how many dollars you and your department or college secure through fund raising or grants, your most important asset will always be the people you serve and the relationships you build. As a leader, always mind your "P's" and "Q's." Prioritize *People* over *Programs* and *Policies* to ensure *Quality*.

Finally, don't let your "first draft be your final draft." We're all a work in progress and should always be willing to learn, adapt, and change. Most importantly, we must be willing to admit when we're wrong. Remember, you will never lead a perfect group of people and they will never have a perfect leader. Therefore, refuse to settle, realizing that none of us ever "arrive" at a place where we can simply go through the motions and expect to grow ourselves and those we serve. How you begin your leadership journey, your first draft, should not be your final draft.

Leading as a department chair can be one of the most rewarding positions we hold in higher education if pursued for the right reasons. In addition, as the leader goes, so goes the organization and its people. Therefore, never stop learning and growing as a leader. In the beginning of this book, I told you that it was my goal to be able to come alongside of you as a colleague and mentor. As a result, I sincerely hope you were able to take something away from these chapters that will be valuable to you, your organization, and, most importantly, those you serve as a leader.

Notes

PREFACE

1. James MacGregor Burns. *Leadership* (New York: Harper & Row, 1978), 2.

CHAPTER 1

1. Walter H. Gmelch and Val D. Miskin. *Department Chair Leadership Skills.* 2nd ed. (Madison, WI: Atwood Publishing, 2011), 5.

2. Gmelch and Miskin, *Department Chair Leadership Skills*, 5.

3. Walter H. Gmelch, Drew Roberts, Kelly Ward, and Sally Hirsch. "A Retrospective View of Department Chairs: Lessons Learned." *The Department Chair* 28, no. 1 (2017): 1–4. https://doi.org/10.1002/dch.30140.

4. Gmelch and Miskin. *Department Chair Leadership Skills*, 5.

5. Walter H. Gmelch, "The Department Chair's Balancing Acts." *New Directions for Higher Education* 2004, no. 126 (2004): 69–84. https://doi.org/10.1002/he.149.

6. Gmelch, "The Department Chai's Balancing Acts," 69–84.

7. Walter H. Gmelch and Jeffrey L. Buller. *Building Academic Leadership Capacity: A Guide to Best Practices* (San Francisco, CA: Jossey-Bass, 2015), 2.

8. Brent Ruben, Richard De Lisi, and Ralph Gigliotti. "Academic Leadership Development Programs: Conceptual Foundations, Structural and Pedagogical Components, and Operational Considerations." *Journal of Leadership Education* 17, no. 3 (2018): 241–54. https://doi.org/10.12806/v17/i3/a5.

9. James MacGregor Burns. *Leadership* (New York: Harper & Row, 1978), 2.

10. Robert E. Cipriano and Richard L. Riccardi. "The Department Chair: A Decade-Long Analysis." *The Department Chair* 28, no. 1 (2017): 11. https://doi.org/10.1002/dch.30144.

11. John C. Maxwell. *Becoming a Person of Influence: How to Positively Impact the Lives of Others*. HarperCollins Leadership, 1997, 17.

12. "You Have to Do Your Own Growing No Matter How Tall Your Grandfather Was." Abraham Lincoln Quote. https://quotefancy.com/quote/18249/Abraham-Lincoln-You-have-to-do-your-own-growing-no-matter-how-tall-your-grandfather-was.

13. Simon Sinek. "How Great Leaders Inspire Action." TED. https://www.ted.com/talks/simon_sinek_how_great_leaders_inspire_action.

14. Simon Sinek, David Mead, and Peter Docker. *Find Your Why: A Practical Guide to Discovering Purpose for You or Your Team* (New York: Portfolio/Penguin, 2017).

15. Sinek et al., *Find Your Why*, 35.

16. Sinek et al., *Find Your Why*, 35.

17. Max De Pree. *Leadership Is an Art* (New York: Currency, 2004), 11.

18. Max Lucado. *When God Whispers Your Name* (Thomas Nelson E-books, 1999), 25.

19. Brené Brown. *Dare to Lead: Brave Work. Tough Conversations. Whole Hearts* (New York: Random House, 2018), 9.

20. Inspiringquotes.us. "Top 14 Quotes of James Lane Allen Famous Quotes and Sayings: Inspringquotes.us." Inspiring Quotes. https://www.inspiringquotes.us/author/1849-james-lane-allen.

CHAPTER 2

1. Clay Scroggins. *How to Lead When You're Not in Charge: Leveraging Influence When You Lack Authority* (Grand Rapids, MI: Zondervan, 2017), 192.

2. "Love." Merriam-Webster. https://www.merriam-webster.com/dictionary/love.

3. Gary D. Chapman and Paul E. White. *The 5 Languages of Appreciation in the Workplace: Empowering Organizations by Encouraging People* (Chicago: Northfield Publishing, 2019).

4. Tom Peters and Robert Waterman. *In Search of Excellence: Lessons from America's Best-Run Companies* (Harper Trade, 1982).

5. Jessica Minahan. "Trauma-Informed Teaching Strategies." http://www.ascd.org/publications/educational_leadership/oct19/vol77/num02/Trauma-Informed_Teaching_Strategies.aspx.

6. "Preventing Adverse Childhood Experiences." Centers for Disease Control and Prevention. https://www.cdc.gov/violenceprevention/aces/fastfact.html?CDC_AA_refVal=https%3A%2F%2Fwww.cdc.gov%2Fviolenceprevention%2Facestudy%2Ffastfact.html.

7. Vincent J. Felitti, Robert F Anda, Dale Nordenberg, David F Williamson, Alison M Spitz, Valerie Edwards, Mary P Koss, and James S Marks. "Relationship of Childhood Abuse and Household Dysfunction to Many of the Leading Causes of Death in Adults." *American Journal of Preventive Medicine* 14, no. 4 (1998): 245–58. https://doi.org/10.1016/s0749-3797(98)00017-8.

8. "Effects of Childhood Trauma on Adults." ISTSS. https://istss.org/public-resources/trauma-basics/what-is-childhood-trauma/effects-of-childhood-trauma.

CHAPTER 3

1. Simon Sinek. *The Infinite Game* (London: Penguin Business, 2020), 95.
2. John C. Maxwell. *Leadershift: The 11 Essential Changes Every Leader Must Embrace* (HarperCollins Leadership, 2019), 19.
3. John Cook and Brandon Vogel. *Dream Like a Champion: Wins, Losses, and Leadership the Nebraska Volleyball Way* (Lincoln: University of Nebraska Press, 2018), 97.
4. Brown, *Dare to Lead*, 9.
5. Stephen R. Covey. *The 7 Habits of Highly Effective People: Powerful Lessons in Personal Change: Restoring the Character Ethic* (New York: Free Press, 2004), 287.
6. Stephen R. Covey. *The 7 Habits of Highly Effective People: Powerful Lessons in Personal Change: Restoring the Character Ethic* (New York: Free Press, 2004), 288.
7. Mark McGraw. "Mastercard CHRO on Anticipating and Adapting to Disruption - i4cp." Institute for Corporate Productivity (i4cp), n.d. https://www.i4cp .com/interviews/mastercard-chro-on-anticipating-and-adapting-to-disruption.

CHAPTER 4

1. Brown, *Dare to Lead*, 4.
2. Brown, *Dare to Lead*, 4.
3. Maciej Duszyński. "A Boss From Hell [2020 Study]." https://resumelab.com/ career-advice/bad-boss.
4. John Grogan, Jocelyn Potter, Anne Collins, and Andy Hopkins. *Marley and Me: Life and Love with the World's Worst Dog* (London: Penguin Books, 2012).
5. Jeffrey L. Buller. *The Essential Department Chair: A Comprehensive Desk Reference* (Hoboken, NJ: Wiley, 2012), 3.
6. Shana Lebowitz. "T. Boone Pickens Asks the Same Question at the Start of His Meetings to Make Sure Every Single Person Comes Prepared." Business Insider, February 27, 2019. https://www.businessinsider.in/t-boone-pickens-asks-the-same -question-at-the-start-of-his-meetings-to-make-sure-every-single-person-comes-pr epared/articleshow/68190021.cms.
7. Sinek, *The Infinite Game*, 129.

CHAPTER 5

1. Max Du Pree. *Leadership Is an Art* (New York: Currency, 2004), 11.
2. "Culture." Merriam-Webster. https://www.merriam-webster.com/dictionary/ culture.
3. John, C. Maxwell, *The Leader's Greatest Return: Attracting, Developing, and Multiplying Leaders* (Thomas Nelson E-books, 2020), 27.

4. "Culture Over Cash? Glassdoor Multi-Country Survey Finds More Than Half of Employees Prioritize Workplace Culture Over Salary." Glassdoor, July 10, 2019. https://www.glassdoor.com/about-us/workplace-culture-over-salary/.

5. Jennifer Robison. "Turning Around Employee Turnover." Gallup.com. Gallup, May 8, 2008. https://news.gallup.com/businessjournal/106912/Turning-Around-Your-Turnover-Problem.aspx.

6. Paul Falcone. *101 Tough Conversations to Have with Employees: A Manager's Guide to Addressing Performance, Conduct, and Discipline Challenges* (New York: HarperCollins Leadership, 2019), 1.

7. Marcel Schwantes. "Want Your Best Workers to Stop Quitting? Start Practicing 3 Habits Found in the Best Managers." Inc.com. Inc., November 20, 2019. https://www.inc.com/marcel-schwantes/want-your-best-workers-to-stop-quitting-start-practicing-3-habits-found-in-best-managers.html.

8. Schwantes. "Want Your Best Workers to Stop Quitting?"

9. Adam Bryant. "Google's Quest to Build a Better Boss." *The New York Times*. March 12, 2011. https://www.nytimes.com/2011/03/13/business/13hire.html?pagewanted=1.

10. Tom Relihan. "Fixing a Toxic Work Culture: Guarding Against the 'Dark Triad'." MIT Sloan, April 29, 2019. https://mitsloan.mit.edu/ideas-made-to-matter/fixing-a-toxic-work-culture-guarding-against-dark-triad.

11. Relihan, "Fixing a Toxic Work Culture."

12. Mariana Bockarova. "Wolves at Work: Machiavellians." *Psychology Today*. Sussex Publishers, September 28, 2020. https://www.psychologytoday.com/us/blog/romantically-attached/202009/wolves-work-machiavellians.

13. *Diagnostic and Statistical Manual of Mental Disorders: DSM-5* (Washington, DC: American Psychiatric Publishing, 2013), 670–71.

14. Bockarova. "Wolves at Work."

15. Scott O. Lilienfeld and Ashley Watts. "Not All Psychopaths Are Criminals – Some Psychopathic Traits Are Actually Linked to Success." *The Conversation*, November 20, 2020. https://theconversation.com/not-all-psychopaths-are-criminals-some-psychopathic-traits-are-actually-linked-to-success-51282.

16. Relihan, "Fixing a Toxic Work Culture."

CHAPTER 6

1. Kevin Oakes. *Culture Renovation: 18 Leadership Actions to Build an Unshakeable Company* (New York, NY: McGraw-Hill, 2021), 97.

2. Oakes, *Culture Renovation*, 20.

CHAPTER 7

1. Heather T. Forbes. *Help for Billy: A Beyond Consequences Approach to Helping Children in the Classroom* (Boulder, CO: Beyond Consequences Institute, 2013), 105.

2. Kevin Oakes. *Culture Renovation: 18 Leadership Actions to Build an Unshakeable Company* (New York: McGraw-Hill, 2021).

3. Craig Groeschel. "Craig Groeschel Leadership Podcast—How to Be Real and Not Be Weird." Life.Church. https://www.life.church/leadershippodcast/how-to-be -real-and-not-be-weird/.

4. Daniel Pink. *Drive: The Surprising Truth About What Motivates Us* (New York: Riverhead Books, 2009), 218.

5. Adam Grant. "Building an Anti-Racist Workplace Transcript." TED, 2021. https://www.ted.com/podcasts/worklife/building-an-anti-racist-workplace-transcript.

CHAPTER 8

1. Punit Saurabh, Prabha Bhola, and Kalyan Kumar Guin. "Reviewing the Knowledge Systems of Innovation and the Associated Roles of Major Stakeholders in the Indian Context." *Technology Innovation Management Review* 4, no. 8 (2014): 36.

2. Merriam-Webster. https://www.merriam-webster.com/dictionary/conflict

3. Merriam-Webster. https://www.merriam-webster.com/dictionary/conflict

4. Merriam-Webster. https://www.merriam-webster.com/dictionary/drama.

5. Victor Hugo. "Things Seen (Choses Vues) V.1." HathiTrust. Accessed March 11, 2021. https://babel.hathitrust.org/cgi/pt?id=mdp.39015008863600&view =1up&seq=102, 102-103.

6. "Overview of Employment Litigation." The United States Department of Justice, February 6, 2021. https://www.justice.gov/crt/overview-employment-li tigation.

7. "Protecting All Students." Title IX. https://sites.ed.gov/titleix/#:~:text=Ti tle%20IX%20was%20enacted%20to,activity%20receiving%20Federal%20financial %20assistance.%E2%80%9D.

8. "TV Interview for Italian Television (RAI)." Margaret Thatcher Foundation, n.d. https://www.margaretthatcher.org/document/106223.

CHAPTER 9

1. Brown, *Dare to Lead*, 92.

2. Christopher Voss and Tahl Raz. *Never Split the Difference: Negotiating as If Your Life Depended on It* (New York: HarperCollins, 2016), 249–56.

3. Voss and Raz. *Never Split the Difference*, 249.

4. Voss and Raz, *Never Split the Difference*, 254.

5. Voss and Raz, *Never Split the Difference*, 54.

6. "The Accusations Audit," https://www.masterclass.com/classes/chris-voss -teaches-the-art-of-negotiation/chapters/the-accusations-audit#:~:text=Chris%20teac hes%20you%20how%20to,and%20turning%20negatives%20into%20positives.&tex

t=Former%20FBI%20lead%20hostage%20negotiator,what%20you%20want%20
every%20day.

7. Voss and Raz, *Never Split the Difference*, 254.

8. Voss and Raz, *Never Split the Difference*, 105.

9. Brandon Voss. "How to Get Buy-in with the 3 Most Effective Communication Techniques." https://blog.blackswanltd.com/the-edge/how-to-get-buy-in-with-the-3 -most-effective-calibrated-questions.

10. Voss and Raz, *Never Split the Difference*, 255–256.

CHAPTER 11

1. "Crisis." Dictionary.com. https://www.dictionary.com/browse/crisis.

2. Max DuPree. *Leadership Is an Art* (New York: Currency, 2004), 11.

3. James C. Collins. *Good to Great: Why Some Companies Make the Leap ... and Others Don't* (New York: HarperCollins, 2009), 83.

4. Collins. *Good to Great*, 85.

5. Kendra Cherry. "Why Toxic Positivity Can Be So Harmful." Verywell Mind, February 1, 2021. https://www.verywellmind.com/what-is-toxic-positivity-509395 8#:~:text=Toxic%20positivity%20is%20the%20belief,should%20maintain%20a%2 0positive%20mindset.

6. "About." Susan David, Ph.D. https://www.susandavid.com/about-susan-d avid#about-the-author.

7. *Brené with Dr. Susan David on the dangers of Toxic Positivity, Part 1 of 2.* (2021, March 1). https://brenebrown.com/podcast/brene-with-dr-susan-david-on-the -dangers-of-toxic-positivity-part-1-of-2/.

8. Joseph Luft and Harrington Ingham. "The Johari Window: A Graphic Model of Interpersonal Awareness." In *Proceedings of the Western Training Laboratory in Group Development* (Los Angeles: UCLA, 1955).

9. Luft and Ingham. "The Johari Window."

10. "There Are Known Knowns." Wikipedia. Wikimedia Foundation, March 29, 2021. https://en.wikipedia.org/wiki/There_are_known_knowns.

11. "Resilience." Merriam-Webster. https://www.merriam-webster.com/dictiona ry/resilience.

12. "Integrity." Dictionary.com. https://www.dictionary.com/browse/integrity.

13. "Strength." Merriam-Webster. https://www.merriam-webster.com/dictionary /strength.

14. "Idiosyncrasy." https://www.dictionary.com/browse/idiosyncrasy.

15. "Ideal." Merriam-Webster. https://www.merriam-webster.com/dictionary/ideal.

CHAPTER 12

1. Laszlo Bock. *Work Rules! Insights from Inside Google That Will Transform How You Live and Lead* (Grand Central Publishing, 2015. Kindle Edition), 67.

2. "A Proud History: The Executive Search Profession and AESC." Accessed March 26, 2021. https://www.aesc.org/insights/magazine/article/proud-history-exec utive-search-profession-and-aesc#:~:text=Indeed%2C%20back%20in%201914 %20Edwin,That's%20what%20really%20matters.

3. Abigail Stewart and Virginia Valian. "Recruiting Diverse and Excellent New Faculty," July 19, 2018. https://www.insidehighered.com/advice/2018/07/19/advice -deans-department-heads-and-search-committees-recruiting-diverse-faculty.

4. Laura Garnett. "The Secret to Hiring an Amazing Employee Requires Doing Something Most Leaders Aren't," May 8, 2017. https://www.inc.com/laura-garnett /the-secret-to-hiring-an-amazing-employee-requires-doing-something-most-leaders -a.html.

5. Shilpa Ahuja. "More Than One-Third Of Workers Would Pass On Perfect Job If Corporate Culture Was Not A Fit, Survey Finds." Media. Accessed March 28, 2021. https://rh-us.mediaroom.com/2018-11-27-More-Than-One-Third-Of-Workers-Would-Pass-On-Perfect-Job-If-Corporate-Culture-Was-Not-A-Fit-Survey-Finds.

6. Trisha Phillips, Kyle R. Saunders, Jeralynn Cossman, and Elizabeth Heitman. "Assessing Trustworthiness in Research: A Pilot Study on CV Verification." *Journal of Empirical Research on Human Research Ethics* 14, no. 4 (2019): 353–64. https:// doi.org/10.1177/1556264619857843.

7. Phillips et al., "Assessing Trustworthiness in Research," 355.

8. Phillips et al., "Assessing Trustworthiness in Research," 358.

9. Courtney Osborn. "Hiring for Culture Fit: The Heart of What We Do." TTA (The Training Associates), December 1, 2020. https://thetrainingassociates.com/h iring-for-culture-fit-the-heart-of-what-we-do/.

CHAPTER 13

1. "About." Garnett Consulting. https://www.lauragarnett.com/about.

2. Laura Garnett. "The 4 Interview Questions That Will Help You Hire the Right People, Every Single Time." Inc.com. Inc., January 13, 2020. https://www.inc.com/ laura-garnett/the-4-interview-questions-that-will-help-you-hire-right-people-every-si ngle-time.html.

3. Garnett. "The 4 Interview Questions."

4. Garnett. "The 4 Interview Questions."

5. Collins, *Good to Great*, 51.

6. "Collegiality." https://www.merriam-webster.com/dictionary/collegiality.

7. Robert E. Cipriano. "Collegiality as a Fourth Criterion for Personnel Decisions." *The Department Chair,* 25, no. 4 (2015): 22. https://doi.org/10.1002/dch .30022.

8. Cipriano, "Collegiality as a Fourth Criterion for Personnel Decisions," 21

9. John Kammeyer-Mueller, Connie Wanberg, Alex Rubenstein, and Zhaoli Song. "Support, Undermining, and Newcomer Socialization: Fitting in During the First 90 Days." *Academy of Management Journal* 56, no. 4 (2013): 1104–24. https:// doi.org/10.5465/amj.2010.0791.

10. Maren Hogan. "How To Get Employee Onboarding Right." *Forbes. Forbes Magazine*, December 2, 2015. https://www.forbes.com/sites/theyec/2015/05/29/how -to-get-employee-onboarding-right/?sh=6e2a028a407b.

11. Nick Otto. "Avoidable Turnover Costing Employers Big." *Employee Benefit News*. August 10, 2017. https://www.benefitnews.com/news/avoidable-turnover -costing-employers-big?brief=00000152-14a7-d1cc-a5fa-7cffccf00000&utm_cont ent=socialflow&utm_campaign=ebnmagazine&utm_source=twitter&utm_medium= social.

12. "Driving Performance and Retention Through Employee Engagement: A Quantitative Analysis of Effective Engagement Strategies." Cooperate Leadership Council, 2004, 5. https://www.achievemission.org/wp-content/uploads/2021/03/Em ployee-Engagement.pdf.

13. "Driving Performance and Retention Through Employee Engagement," 43.

14. Kammeyer-Mueller et al., "Support, Undermining, and Newcomer Socialization," 1104–24.

15. Dawn Klinghoffer, Candice Young, and Xue Liu. "To Retain New Hires, Make Sure You Meet with Them in Their First Week," August 28, 2018. https://hbr .org/2018/06/to-retain-new-hires-make-sure-you-meet-with-them-in-their-first-week.

16. Klinghoffer et al., "To Retain New Hires,"

17. Talya Bauer. *Onboarding New Employees: Maximizing Success*. SHRM Foundation, 2010, 2. https://www.shrm.org/foundation/ourwork/initiatives/resources -from-past-initiatives/Documents/Onboarding%20New%20Employees.pdf.

18. Bauer, *Onboarding New Employees: Maximizing Success*.

19. "Employee Offboarding," November 22, 2020. https://en.wikipedia.org/wiki/ Employee_offboarding.

20. Scott D. Clary. "It Takes 20 Years to Build a Reputation and Five Minutes to Ruin It." Medium. Medium, July 5, 2020. https://scottdclary.medium.com/it-takes-20 -years-to-build-a-reputation-and-five-minutes-to-ruin-it-ecbbf58fb6ef.

CHAPTER 14

1. George D. Kuh. *High-Impact Educational Practices: What They Are, Who Has Access to Them, and Why They Matter*. (Association of American Colleges and Universities), 2008.

2. Krista M. Soria and Matthew Johnson. "High-Impact Educational Practices and the
Development of College Students' Pluralistic Outcomes." *College Student Affairs Journal* 35, no. 2 (Fall 2017): 102

3. Kuh, *High-Impact Educational Practices*, 9–11.

4. Kuh, *High-Impact Educational Practices*, 10.

5. Kuh, *High-Impact Educational Practices*, 10.

6. Krista M. Soria and Matthew Johnson. "High-Impact Educational Practices and the Development of College Students' Pluralistic Outcomes." *College Student Affairs Journal* 35, no. 2 (Fall 2017): 100.

CHAPTER 15

1. Gmelch and Miskin, *Department Chair Leadership Skills*, 153.
2. Gmelch and Miskin, *Department Chair Leadership Skills*, 152.
3. Brown, *Dare to Lead*, 4.
4. Anthony K. Tjan. "What the Best Mentors Do," December 5, 2017. https://hb r.org/2017/02/what-the-best-mentors-do.
5. Tjan. "What the Best Mentors Do."
6. Rodger Duncan. "Titles Don't Make Leaders," August 27, 2018. https://www .forbes.com/sites/rodgerdeanduncan/2018/08/25/titles-dont-make-leaders/?sh=5d45 21b86021.
7. Kevin N. Lawrence. *Your Oxygen Mask First: 17 Habits to Help High Achievers Survive & Thrive in Leadership & Life* (Austin, TX: Lioncrest Publishing, 2017), 205.
8. "Legacy." Merriam-Webster. https://www.merriam-webster.com/dictionary/le gacy#synonyms.

CONCLUSION

1. Buller, *The Essential Department Chair*, 3.
2. Sinek, *The Infinite Game*, 32.
3. Sinek, *The Infinite Game*, 33.

Bibliography

"A Proud History: The Executive Search Profession And AESC.". https://www
.aesc.org/insights/magazine/article/proud-history-executive-search-profession-and
-aesc#:~:text=Indeed%2C%20back%20in%201914%20Edwin,That's%20what%2
0really%20matters.

"About." Garnett Consulting. https://www.lauragarnett.com/about.

"About." Susan David, Ph.D. https://www.susandavid.com/about-susan-david#about
-the-author.

Ahuja, Shilpa. "More Than One-Third of Workers Would Pass on Perfect Job If
Corporate Culture Was Not a Fit, Survey Finds." Media. Accessed March 28, 2021.
https://rh-us.mediaroom.com/2018-11-27-More-Than-One-Third-Of-Workers
-Would-Pass-On-Perfect-Job-If-Corporate-Culture-Was-Not-A-Fit-Survey-Finds.

Bauer, Talya. *Onboarding New Employees: Maximizing Success*. SHRM Foundation,
2010. https://www.shrm.org/foundation/ourwork/initiatives/resources-from-past
-initiatives/Documents/Onboarding%20New%20Employees.pdf.

Bock, Laszlo. *Work Rules! Insights from Inside Google That Will Transform How
You Live and Lead*. Grand Central Publishing, 2015. Kindle Edition.

Bockarova, Mariana. "Wolves at Work: Machiavellians." Psychology Today.
Sussex Publishers, September 28, 2020. https://www.psychologytoday.com/us/
blog/romantically-attached/202009/wolves-work-machiavellians.

Brené with Dr. Susan David on the Dangers of Toxic Positivity, Part 1 of 2. (2021,
March 1). https://brenebrown.com/podcast/brene-with-dr-susan-david-on-the-dan-
gers-of-toxic-positivity-part-1-of-2/.

Brown, Brené. *Dare to Lead: Brave Work. Tough Conversations. Whole Hearts*. New
York: Random House, 2018.

Bryant, Adam. "Google's Quest to Build a Better Boss." The New York Times,
March 12, 2011. https://www.nytimes.com/2011/03/13/business/13hire.html
?pagewanted=1.

Burns, James MacGregor. *Leadership*. New York: Harper & Row, 1978.

Buller, Jeffrey L. *The Essential Department Chair: A Comprehensive Desk Reference.* Hoboken, NJ: Wiley, 2012.

Chapman, Gary D., and Paul E. White. *The 5 Languages of Appreciation in the Workplace: Empowering Organizations by Encouraging People.* Chicago: Northfield Publishing, 2019.

Cherry, Kendra. "Why Toxic Positivity Can Be So Harmful." Verywell Mind, February 1, 2021. https://www.verywellmind.com/what-is-toxic-posi-tivity-5093958#:~:text=Toxic%20positivity%20is%20the%20belief,should%20maintain%20a%20positive%20mindset.

Cipriano, Robert E. "Collegiality as a Fourth Criterion for Personnel Decisions." *The Department Chair,* 25, no. 4 (2015): 22. https://doi.org/10.1002/dch.30022.

Cipriano, Robert E., and Richard L. Riccardi. "The Department Chair: A Decade-Long Analysis". *The Department Chair* 28, no. 1 (2017): 1–4.

Clary, Scott D. "It Takes 20 Years to Build a Reputation and Five Minutes to Ruin It." Medium. Medium, July 5, 2020. https://scottdclary.medium.com/it-takes-20-years-to-build-a-reputation-and-five-minutes-to-ruin-it-ecbbf58fb6ef.

"Collegiality." https://www.merriam-webster.com/dictionary/collegiality.

Collins, James C. *Good to Great: Why Some Companies Make the Leap ... and Others Don't.* New York: HarperCollins, 2009.

"Conflict." Merriam-Webster. https://www.merriam-webster.com/dictionary/conflict

Cook, John, and Brandon Vogel. *Dream like a Champion: Wins, Losses, and Leadership the Nebraska Volleyball Way.* Lincoln: University of Nebraska Press, 2018.

Covey, Stephen R. *The 7 Habits of Highly Effective People: Powerful Lessons in Personal Change: Restoring the Character Ethic.* New York: Free Press, 2004.

"Crisis." Dictionary.com. Dictionary.com. https://www.dictionary.com/browse/crisis.

"Culture." Merriam-Webster. Merriam-Webster. https://www.merriam-`webster.com/dictionary/culture.

"Culture Eats Strategy for Breakfast." The Management Centre, April 23, 2020. https://www.managementcentre.co.uk/management-consultancy/culture-eats-strat-egy-for-breakfast/#:~:text=%E2%80%9CCulture%20eats%20strategy%20for%20breakfast,surer%20route%20to%20organisational%20success.

"Culture Over Cash? Glassdoor Multi-Country Survey Finds More Than Half of Employees Prioritize Workplace Culture Over Salary." Glassdoor, July 10, 2019. https://www.glassdoor.com/about-us/workplace-culture-over-salary/.

Diagnostic and Statistical Manual of Mental Disorders: DSM-5. Washington, DC: American Psychiatric Publishing, 2013.

"Drama." Merriam-Webster. https://www.merriam-webster.com/dictionary/drama.

"Driving Performance and Retention Through Employee Engagement: A Quantitative Analysis of Effective Engagement Strategies." Cooperate Leadership Council, 2004. https://www.achievemission.org/wp-content/uploads/2021/03/Employee-Engagement.pdf.

Duncan, Rodger. "Titles Don't Make Leaders," August 27, 2018. https://www.forbes.com/sites/rodgerdeanduncan/2018/08/25/titles-dont-make-leaders/?sh=5d4521b86021.

DuPree, Max. *Leadership Is an Art.* New York: Currency, 2004.

Duszyński, Maciej. "A Boss From Hell [2020 Study]." https://resumelab.com/career -advice/bad-boss.

Edwards, Valerie, Mary P. Koss and James S. Marks "Relationship of Childhood Abuse and Household Dysfunction to Many of the Leading Causes of Death in Adults." *American Journal of Preventive Medicine* 14, no. 4 (1998): 245–58. https://doi.org/10.1016/s0749-3797(98)00017-8.

"Effects of Childhood Trauma on Adults." ISTSS. https://istss.org/public-resources/ trauma-basics/what-is-childhood-trauma/effects-of-childhood-trauma.

"Employee Offboarding," November 22, 2020. https://en.wikipedia.org/wiki/ Employee_offboarding.

Falcone, Paul. *101 Tough Conversations to Have with Employees: A Manager's Guide to Addressing Performance, Conduct, and Discipline Challenges*. New York: HarperCollins Leadership, 2019.

Felitti, Vincent J., Robert F. Anda, Dale Nordenberg, David F. Williamson, Alison M. Spitz, Valerie Edwards, Mary P. Koss, and James S. Marks. "Relationship of Childhood Abuse and Household Dysfunction to Many of the Leading Causes of Death in Adults." *American Journal of Preventive Medicine* 14, no. 4 (1998): 245–58. https://doi.org/10.1016/s0749-3797(98)00017-8.

Forbes, Heather T. *Help for Billy: a Beyond Consequences Approach to Helping Children in the Classroom*. Boulder, CO: Beyond Consequences Institute, 2013, 105.

Garnett, Laura. "The 4 Interview Questions That Will Help You Hire the Right People, Every Single Time." Inc.com. Inc., January 13, 2020. https://www.inc .com/laura-garnett/the-4-interview-questions-that-will-help-you-hire-right-people -every-single-time.html.

Garnett, Laura. "The Secret to Hiring an Amazing Employee Requires Doing Something Most Leaders Aren't," May 8, 2017. https://www.inc.com/laura-garnett/the-secret-to -hiring-an-amazing-employee-requires-doing-something-most-leaders-a.html.

Gmelch, Walter H. "The Department Chair's Balancing Acts." *New Directions for Higher Education* 2004, no. 126 (2004): 69–84. https://doi.org/10.1002/he.149.

Gmelch, Walter H., Drew Roberts, Kelly Ward, and Sally Hirsch. "A Retrospective View of Department Chairs: Lessons Learned." *The Department Chair* 28, no 1 (2017): 1–4.

Gmelch, Walter H., and Jeffrey L. Buller. *Building Academic Leadership Capacity: A Guide to Best Practices*. San Francisco, CA: Jossey-Bass, 2015.

Gmelch, Walter H., and Val D. Miskin. *Department Chair Leadership Skills*. 2nd ed. Madison, WI: Atwood Publishing, 2011, 5.

Grant, Adam. "Building an Anti-Racist Workplace Transcript." TED, 2021. https:// www.ted.com/podcasts/worklife/building-an-anti-racist-workplace-transcript.

Groeschel, Craig. "Craig Groeschel Leadership Podcast - How to Be Real and Not Be Weird." Life. Church. https://www.life.church/leadershippodcast/how-to-be-real -and-not-be-weird/.

Grogan, John, Jocelyn Potter, Anne Collins, and Andy Hopkins. *Marley and Me: Life and Love with the World's Worst Dog*. London: Penguin Books, 2012.

Hogan, Maren. "How To Get Employee Onboarding Right." Forbes. Forbes Magazine, December 2, 2015. https://www.forbes.com/sites/theyec/2015/05/29/ how-to-get-employee-onboarding-right/?sh=6e2a028a407b.

Hugo, V. "Things Seen (Choses Vues) V.1." HathiTrust. https://babel.hathitrust.org/cgi/pt?id=mdp.39015008863600&view=1up&seq=102

"Ideal." Merriam-Webster. Merriam-Webster. https://www.merriam-webster.com/dictionary/ideal.

"Idiosyncrasy." https://www.dictionary.com/browse/idiosyncrasy.

Inspiringquotes.us. "Top 14 Quotes of James Lane Allen Famous Quotes and Sayings: Inspringquotes.us." Inspiring Quotes. https://www.inspiringquotes.us/author/1849-james-lane-allen.

Lincoln Quote. https://quotefancy.com/quote/18249/Abraham-Lincoln-You-have-to-do-your-own-growing-no-matter-how-tall-your-grandfather-was.

"Integrity." Dictionary.com. Dictionary.com. https://www.dictionary.com/browse/integrity.

Kammeyer-Mueller, John, Connie Wanberg, Alex Rubenstein, and Zhaoli Song. "Support, Undermining, and Newcomer Socialization: Fitting in During the First 90 Days." *Academy of Management Journal* 56, no. 4 (2013): 1104–24. https://doi.org/10.5465/amj.2010.0791.

Klinghoffer, Dawn, Candice Young, and Xue Liu. "To Retain New Hires, Make Sure You Meet with Them in Their First Week," August 28, 2018. https://hbr.org/2018/06/to-retain-new-hires-make-sure-you-meet-with-them-in-their-first-week.

Kuh, George D. *High-Impact Educational Practices: What They Are, Who Has Access to Them, and Why They Matter.* Association of American Colleges and Universities, 2008.

Lawrence, Kevin N. *Your Oxygen Mask First: 17 Habits to Help High Achievers Survive & Thrive in Leadership & Life.* Austin, TX: Lioncrest Publishing, 2017.

Lebowitz, Shana. "T. Boone Pickens Asks the Same Question at the Start of His Meetings to Make Sure Every Single Person Comes Prepared." Business Insider, February 27, 2019. https://www.businessinsider.in/t-boone-pickens-asks-the-same-question-at-the-start-of-his-meetings-to-make-sure-every-single-person-comes-prepared/articleshow/68190021.cms.

"Legacy." Merriam-Webster. Merriam-Webster.https://www.merriam-webster.com/dictionary/legacy#synonyms.

Lilienfeld, Scott O, and Ashley Watts . "Not All Psychopaths Are Criminals – Some Psychopathic Traits Are Actually Linked to Success." The Conversation, November 20, 2020. https://theconversation.com/not-all-psychopaths-are-criminals-some-psychopathic-traits-are-actually-linked-to-success-51282.

"Love." Merriam-Webster. Merriam-Webster. https://www.merriam-webster.com/dictionary/love.

Lucado, Max. *When God Whispers Your Name.* Thomas Nelson E-books, 1999.

Luft, Joseph, and Harrington Ingham. "The Johari Window: A Graphic Model of Interpersonal Awareness." In *Proceedings of the Western Training Laboratory in Group Development.* Los Angeles: UCLA, 1955.

Maxwell, John, C. *The Leader's Greatest Return: Attracting, Developing, and Multiplying Leaders.* Thomas Nelson E-books, 2020.

Maxwell, John C. *Leadershift: The 11 Essential Changes Every Leader Must Embrace*. HarperCollins Leadership, 2019.

Maxwell, John C. *Becoming a Person of Influence: How to Positively Impact the Lives of Others*. HarperCollins Leadership, 1997.

McGraw, Mark. "Mastercard CHRO on Anticipating and Adapting to Disruption - i4cp." Institute for Corporate Productivity (i4cp), n.d. https://www.i4cp.com/ interviews/mastercard-chro-on-anticipating-and-adapting-to-disruption.

Minahan, Jessica. "Trauma-Informed Teaching Strategies." http://www.ascd.org/pub- lications/educational_leadership/oct19/vol77/num02/Trauma-Informed_Teaching _Strategies.aspx.

Oakes, Kevin. *Culture Renovation: 18 Leadership Actions to Build an Unshakeable Company*. New York: McGraw-Hill, 2021.

Osborn, Courtney. "Hiring for Culture Fit: The Heart of What We Do." TTA (The Training Associates), December 1, 2020. https://thetrainingassociates.com/hiring -for-culture-fit-the-heart-of-what-we-do/.

Otto, Nick. "Avoidable Turnover Costing Employers Big." Employee Benefit News. Employee Benefit News, August 10, 2017. https://www.benefitnews.com/news/ avoidable-turnover-costing-employers-big?brief=00000152-14a7-d1cc-a5fa-7cff- ccf00000&utm_content=socialflow&utm_campaign=ebnmagazine&utm_source =twitter&utm_medium=social.

"Overview of Employment Litigation." The United States Department of Justice, February 6, 2021. https://www.justice.gov/crt/overview-employment-litigation.

Peters, Tom., and Robert Waterman. *In Search of Excellence: Lessons from America's Best-Run Companies*. Harper Trade, 1982.

Phillips, Trisha, Kyle R Saunders, Jeralynn Cossman, and Elizabeth Heitman. "Assessing Trustworthiness in Research: A Pilot Study on CV Verification." *Journal of Empirical Research on Human Research Ethics* 14, no. 4 (2019): 353–64. https://doi.org/10.1177/1556264619857843.

Pink, Daniel. *Drive: The Surprising Truth About What Motivates Us*. New York: Riverhead Books, 2009.

"Preventing Adverse Childhood Experiences." Centers for Disease Control and Prevention. https://www.cdc.gov/violenceprevention/aces/fastfact.html?CDC_AA _refVal=https%3A%2F%2Fwww.cdc.gov%2Fviolenceprevention%2Facestudy %2Ffastfact.html.

Relihan, Tom. "Fixing a Toxic Work Culture: Guarding Against the 'Dark Triad.'" MIT Sloan, April 29, 2019. https://mitsloan.mit.edu/ideas-made-to-matter/fixing-a -toxic-work-culture-guarding-against-dark-triad.

Robison, Jennifer. "Turning Around Employee Turnover." Gallup.com. Gallup, May 8, 2008. https://news.gallup.com/businessjournal/106912/Turning-Around-Your -Turnover-Problem.aspx.

Ruben, Brent, Richard De Lisi, and Ralph Gigliotti. "Academic Leadership Development Programs: Conceptual Foundations, Structural and Pedagogical Components, and Operational Considerations." *Journal of Leadership Education* 17, no. 3 (2018): 241–54. https://doi.org/10.12806/v17/i3/a5.

Saurabh, Punit, Prabha Bhola, and Kalyan Kumar Guin. "Reviewing the Knowledge Systems of Innovation and the Associated Roles of Major Stakeholders in the Indian Context." *Technology Innovation Management Review* 4, no. 8 (2014): 36–45.

Schwantes, Marcel. "Want Your Best Workers to Stop Quitting? Start Practicing 3 Habits Found in the Best Managers." Inc.com. Inc., November 20, 2019. https://www.inc.com/marcel-schwantes/want-your-best-workers-to-stop-quitting-start-practicing-3-habits-found-in-best-managers.html.

Scroggins, Clay. *How to Lead When You're Not in Charge: Leveraging Influence When You Lack Authority.* Grand Rapids, MI: Zondervan, 2017.

Sinek, Simon. "How Great Leaders Inspire Action." TED. https://www.ted.com/talks/simon_sinek_how_great_leaders_inspire_action.

Sinek, Simon. *The Infinite Game.* London: Penguin Business, 2020.

Sinek, Simon, David Mead, and Peter Docker. *Find Your Why: A Practical Guide to Discovering Purpose for You or Your Team.* New York, NY: Portfolio/Penguin, 2017.

Soria, Krista M., and Matthew Johnson. "High-Impact Educational Practices and the Development of College Students' Pluralistic Outcomes." *College Student Affairs Journal* 35, no. 2 (Fall 2017): 100–116.

Stewart, Abigail, and Valian, Virginia. "Recruiting Diverse and Excellent New Faculty," July 19, 2018. https://www.insidehighered.com/advice/2018/07/19/advice-deans-department-heads-and-search-committees-recruiting-diverse-faculty.

"Strength." Merriam-Webster. Merriam-Webster. https://www.merriam-webster.com/dictionary/strength. "The Accusations Audit," https://www.masterclass.com/classes/chris-voss-teaches-the-art-of-negotiation/chapters/the-accusations-audit#:~:text=Chris%20teaches%20you%20how%20to,and%20turning%20negatives%20into%20positives.&text=Former%20FBI%20lead%20hostage%20negotiator, what%20you%20want%20every%20day.

"There Are Known Knowns." Wikipedia. Wikimedia Foundation, March 29, 2021. https://en.wikipedia.org/wiki/There_are_known_knowns.

Tjan, Anthony K. "What the Best Mentors Do," December 5, 2017. https://hbr.org/2017/02/what-the-best-mentors-do.

"TV Interview for Italian Television (RAI)." Margaret Thatcher Foundation, n.d. https://www.margaretthatcher.org/document/106223.

Voss, Brandon. "How to Get Buy-in with the 3 Most Effective Communication Techniques." https://blog.blackswanltd.com/the-edge/how-to-get-buy-in-with-the-3-most-effective-calibrated-questions.

Voss, Christopher, and Tahl Raz. *Never Split the Difference: Negotiating as If Your Life Depended on It.* New York: HarperCollins, 2016.

"'You Have to Do Your Own Growing No Matter How Tall Your Grandfather Was.'" Abraham Lincoln Quote. https://quotefancy.com/quote/18249/Abraham-Lincoln-You-have-to-do-your-own-growing-no-matter-how-tall-your-grandfather-was

About the Author

Dr. Christopher J. Jochum currently serves as the chair of the Teacher Education Department at Fort Hays State University (Hays, KS) where he leads a large teacher preparation program with over 1,000 students. As a former public school teacher with fifteen years of experience working in higher education, Dr. Jochum has worked with his colleagues to create new programs and policies designed to increase student engagement, retention, and success.

Made in the USA
Coppell, TX
03 July 2024